Deconstructing the NYSTCE for the **ALST**

Deconstructing the NYSTCE for the ALST

Written and Compiled
by Bridgette Gubernatis

Additional editing and research
by Aurdrea Weiman

Copyright © 2016 by Bridgette Gubernatis.

| ISBN: | Softcover | 978-1-5144-3101-6 |
| | eBook | 978-1-5144-3102-3 |

All rights reserved. No part of this book may be reproduced or transmitted in any form or by any means, electronic or mechanical, including photocopying, recording, or by any information storage and retrieval system, without permission in writing from the copyright owner.

Any people depicted in stock imagery provided by Thinkstock are models, and such images are being used for illustrative purposes only.
Certain stock imagery © Thinkstock.

Print information available on the last page.

Rev. date: 01/20/2016

To order additional copies of this book, contact:
Xlibris
1-888-795-4274
www.Xlibris.com
Orders@Xlibris.com
730088

Table of Contents

Why is this book different?	ix
The Turning Point for Me as a Test Prep Teacher for the NYSTCE	xiii
PART 1: THE ESSAYS	1
Deconstructing the Types of Essays	1
Essay 1	5
Common mistakes that test takers make	6
Essay 2	11
Understanding the Charts & Essay 2	14
Types of Charts	24
Essay 3: The Argumentative Essay	41
Which Side Should I Take?	42
Deconstructing the Essay by Paragraph	47
FIVE and FIVE strategy	52
Common Mistakes that Writers Make in the Introduction	54
Understanding a "Strong" argument	59
Understanding Money Arguments	65
Extending the Argument	73
Paragraph 4: The Counter Claim	77
The Conclusion	80
Rubric for Essay 3	86

PART 2: HOW TO FAIL YOUR ESSAYS!	87
Alligator Blood!	87
Not Baking the Cookies!	91
Thesaurus Trolls!!!	94
Drama Queens!!!	96
Tips to Help You Stay Organized	99
Generalities of Writing Mistakes by American and ESOL Writers	105
PART 3: THE MULTIPLE CHOICE	115
Dead White Men	118
Era and Dates	122
Diversity	130
Types of Reading Comprehension Passages	136

Acknowledgements

This book would not be possible without the support of many people. Many thanks to the students I have had over the years who have taught me much more than I have ever taught them. Teaching educators is one of the things in my life of which I am most proud.

I want to thank the teachers I have had in my own life who have inspired a love of learning in me. That flame, once lit, never dies. I have had more than my fair share. Thank you to Elizabeth Davis Kolodny and her husband David, Barbara Shekore, Patty Dimaio Simon, R. Christopher Wilde, Audrey Cheek and the elusive Ms. Saroka.

I would also like to thank a team of people who have helped me to develop these classes and strategies over the years including Carmine Mucciarone, Eloy Cruz Bizet, Jamie Russel and Aurdrea Weiman. And the team at TRS: Nasser, James and Anwar. We are helping to change the world one teacher at a time, and we love it.

Why is this book different?

Every time I have been motivated to write a new study guide it is because students have brought an over-priced completely unhelpful study guide into my class and I get annoyed that someone is confusing test takers and trying make money off them in the process.

The difference between my study guides is that they are based on psychometric evaluation of students taking the actual test. What is psychometrics? It's the study of testing and how people operate when they are taking tests: how they react emotionally, psychologically and cognitively. I am less interested in what makes a person do great on a test and more interested in why they fail.

I have taught the NYSTCE test prep exclusively every week for the last 7 years and so I've had the opportunity to see the kinds of mistakes test takers are making on the test and why they are failing. I often ask students this question, "How many times have you failed the test?" Most people will say a few times. I on the other hand have "failed it" hundreds of times through my students and so I have come to realize the kinds of things people do wrong on the test. Don't worry, I've also "passed it" ten times more than I've "failed it" through the students. Over the years I have taught thousands of students to pass the tests for the NYSTCE. I know how you THINK and why it confuses you on the test.

This study guide is written based on my classroom instruction. Obviously we cannot put in actual questions or topics that may show up on the test. Instead we'll choose topics for the Essay and questions for the Reading

Comprehension section that are similar to what you will see on the exam. Please keep this in mind. They are **similar** but **different.**

I caution students to be wary of "test prep" that is prepared by English teachers doing this on the side. I believe the passing score for the ALST is an 86.6%. You cannot teach a timed standardized test the same way you can teach someone to write an English paper. In fact, most of the students I get in my classes are students who had previously taken a workshop taught by an English teacher. I myself have a background in English; my major in my undergraduate degree was English.

I would never teach an English class the way I teach test prep because it is an entirely different way of doing things. When students write a paper for an English class they have time to edit it and work on it. They are able to "revise a rough draft" and then submit the final draft for evaluation.

On a timed exam you have to be able to write the entire essay off the top of your head. The only way to practice doing it is to write out your first version of the essay. On this version you likely spent a few hours or days writing and revising. You will then need to sit down and time yourself to rewrite the entire thing off the top of your head *without looking at your original draft.* This is the key difference between how English teachers teach and how test prep teachers teach.

During this writing you should set a timer for 1 hour so that you are experiencing the time constraints you will face on the test. Then you edit. Then you do it again and again and again. You cannot simply write a draft and fix it up and think you are good to go for the test.

This test prep guide will be broken into three sections. The first two parts will be about the essay and the third part will be about the Reading Comprehension Multiple Choice. Keep in mind that **the essays are 60% of the test.** Don't get caught up in the multiple choice thinking they are the key to passing the test. They are not. I have regularly had students show up in the class with 3 pluses on the Multiple Choice and a failing score on the essay. Most students already do well on the Multiple Choice but they still fail the test because they ran out of time on the essays. The key to passing the test is passing the essays, not the Multiple Choice.

Also please note: I have made this study guide small and compact so that you can stick it in a bag and read it easily. I have also used a larger font to make sure it is easily read by people with vision issues. This is not done to "pad the book" but to make this book as accessible as possible. I am also trying to keep it short, because the last thing you need is tons of material to read to understand.

The formatting in the book is designed for ease of reading, especially in sections that have charts or bullet points. So you may find extra white space that was necessary to keep the layout clear. I want this to be an easy to use study guide.

And, note, in this book ALL NAMES of former students have been changed. *

The Turning Point for Me as a Test Prep Teacher for the NYSTCE

Before we begin I want to share a bit about myself and my experiences working with teachers on the NYSTCE. As I have noted before, I now teach this test exclusively. I used to teach the SAT, ACT, GRE, ASVAB and other types of test prep. Then I moved onto the NYSTCE tests because I had to take them myself even though I never actually became a certified teacher. I started working with several different companies doing the NYSTCE part time. Then I started working for BEC and soon I had no time to teach anything other than the NYSTCE.

In this time I've gotten to know teachers. I've watched you struggle. I've seen how some teachers are working full time and going to school at night. Then going home to family responsibilities and your own children. I honestly don't know how you do it. I've watched you struggle with finances and max out credit cards paying for the tests only to fail and have to pay again with money you can't afford. I've watched you succeed and cheered on your accomplishments. I've watched you fail and cry. And I used to rally you by saying, "Stop crying. Get mad! Fight!" That's because in my opinion the tests are unfair and expensive. Don't let it work its way into your psyche. Don't let them beat you down. Keep going. You will get there.

At one point in my teaching I started trying to encourage my female teachers to "think like a guy! Men don't cry, men get mad because they are annoyed about wasting their money! They think "That could have been Knicks tickets!" They don't think "I'm a terrible teacher! I'm an idiot!" They don't let it get to them.

I used to make teachers watch a video clip from the movie "A League of Their Own," the one where Tom Hanks yells at the young woman for crying and says "There's no crying in baseball!" My teachers would laugh and regroup and go pass the test. I'd tell my teachers "I'm not a ballet teacher, I'm a soccer coach. What's the difference between a ballet teacher and a soccer coach? The soccer coach wants to win!" And I'd stay with you until you passed. I'd tell you that if you didn't pass I'd break yer kneecaps! Come on now! Let's do it! And we always did.

I still say some of these things to my teachers. But one day a turning point happened. I still cannot talk about this day without becoming overwhelmed. It was the most humbling moment of my career. It really woke me up to the amount of pressure you are under and I realized that you yourselves do not realize how much pressure you are under either. It's only when you come out from under it that you do realize.

I vividly remember the morning. Sunlight streaming in the windows, it was a day I had gotten up early. My youngest son was off to school. I was going through emails and drinking coffee. I have profound hearing loss, (100 percent deaf in one ear and only 20% hearing in the other, it's part of why I don't teach in a school. I wouldn't be able to do it every day.) Because of this I don't have a cell phone, but on this day my son had left his cell phone at home, sitting on my desk.

The regular phone rang and when I picked up the phone someone was sobbing on the other end of the phone. And when I say sobbing, I mean deep punctuated sobs and the person couldn't get words out. I was actually frightened and thought someone had accidentally called me instead of calling 911. I kept asking who it was: "Who is it? Are you ok? What's going on?" Still no answer, just choking sobs. I got even more worried and grabbed my son's phone ready to dial 911 and I started yelling into the phone at this point, "Tell me your address! Just tell me your address! I'll call 911." Finally the person spoke. "It's me Bridgette, it's Marcus*"

Marcus was a teacher who had taken the CST Students with Disabilities about 10 times and couldn't pass it. He kept missing it by one or two points. Finally he had come to my class. It was his last chance before the tests changed. He'd already been told he'd be let go from his job if he couldn't pass. They'd keep him on as a substitute, but he'd be losing his insurance and making a fraction of his salary. His house was already close to foreclosure and he desperately needed to pass. He had two small children and his wife worked as well, but it just wouldn't be enough.

Immediately my heart seized up with fear. The scores had come out the night before. Oh no! "What happened Marcus? What happened, what's wrong?" He finally was able to get out the words, "I passed! I finally passed. It's over." For the next five minutes he sat there sobbing with me on the phone. And of course I started crying too. He poured out such a tremendous amount of gratitude that I started to feel uncomfortable because it was so humbling.

Then I started feeling something else creep in that changed me. I started getting really, really angry. I remember a growing fire in my heart that said, "No one should ever have this kind of a reaction to passing a standardized test!" It was unbelievable to me that Marcus, who had taught for years in the classroom was essentially being told he was "suddenly not good enough." Really? So one day he's fine and he's a great teacher. But the next day he is not "qualified" and he's got to go! Oh but you'll keep him in the classroom of course, doing the exact same job, only paying a fraction of the salary. How is this in any way ethical or fair?

How does "one test" make the difference between a good teacher and a bad teacher? How does a school system, that asks you to learn how to do differentiated instruction, assess the ability of a teacher by using a standardized exam? The fact that the students are learning, the fact that Marcus is amazing, the fact that he is dedicated, all that doesn't matter? It's the test? That's what matters? Really? Seriously?

That day was a turning point for me as a test prep teacher. It made me understand what was at stake and how much schools need teachers like Marcus to be in the classroom. Not just the ones who can pass the tests easily. That's because not all *students* can pass tests easily and a teacher who has struggled themselves will be a much more understanding teacher.

Many of the teachers I teach are the most devoted and dedicated teachers that we wish all our children could have as teachers. I get the best in my classroom and it reminds me of what the system is really like. The good ones struggle to keep up with standardized testing. The creative ones are left behind. Only those who know how to stoically play the game get through easily. But the ones who should be there often fall between the cracks. So I take back what I said before. Men do cry.

All good teachers cry.

All good teachers cry at some point in their careers. I'm just blessed beyond belief that I get to hear the tears of joy. Yeah, there's no crying in baseball, except sometimes there is. And it's Victory! Thanks for letting me be the coach that shares it with you.

And love to you Marcus, for helping me grow. You know who you are.

PART 1: THE ESSAYS

Deconstructing the Types of Essays

One of the biggest problems teachers have on the essays is that, because they are in graduate school, they have gotten used to two types of writing: Lesson Plans and Term Papers. On this test you are being asked to write three different TYPES of Essays.

Essay 1 is an ***Expository Essay.*** You explain what the two writers have said.

Essay 2 is an ***Analytical Essay.*** You analyze data in a chart and a writer's statements.

Essay 3 is an ***Argumentative Essay.*** You write an opinionated essay. This essay is very similar to a persuasive essay. What is the difference between an argumentative essay and a persuasive essay?

In a persuasive essay you argue your opinion. In an argumentative essay you argue your opinion *as opposed to those of others.* In other words you are arguing against the statements in Passage A and/or Passage B. You are fighting against someone for your point. A lot of test takers think you are supposed to be "agreeing with one side" but that is not necessarily an argumentative essay. What's the key word here? ARGUMENT not AGREEMENT.

In my experience many teachers don't know how to write opinionated essays very well after going into teaching. Why? Well in many ways teachers are trained not to ever give their real opinion on anything. They are taught to be "diplomatic" and "nice" when talking to parents or students. They are almost brainwashed to do the opposite of arguing.

Think about the last time you had a parent teacher conference. Probably at one point you wanted to say *"You know, the problem with this student is that you are a lazy parent who doesn't support your child in completing their work. You expect us to do everything while you do nothing. Then you whine because he isn't doing well in school!"*

Do you say this? Of course not. Instead you say something like this: *"Your son is an enthusiastic learner, but he needs support to be able to complete his assignments on time. Let's create some learning strategies to help reach this goal."* You smile and pretend you aren't really annoyed.

Or you wanted to say, *"Maybe if you taught your child some discipline and respect he wouldn't disrupt the entire classroom by jumping out of his seat all the time? Instead of dumping your kid in front of a television set why not work with him after school?"*

Do you say this? Of course not. Instead you say something like this. *"Your son is very sociable but he has difficulty staying on task. Let's work on some strategies to help him stay focused."* And again you smile and pretend you are not really annoyed.

If you do this long enough you start to slip away from your voice in writing. You feel that your writing should explain things and be diplomatic. But that is not what you need to be doing in Essay 3. You need to be taking a strong opinionated side in a debate.

This is what I mean when I say that "I know how you THINK." I will be explaining the rules of the tests to you but also explaining why you get confused. Perhaps it doesn't apply to everyone but it's what I've seen that confuses most test takers that come to my classes. If it doesn't apply to you just bear with me and try to see the point.

Think about the last time you turned in a "paper" for school. How long was it? Probably several pages. You are used to having a lot of writing to be able to clarify your points. On this test the word counts are very low: Essay 1 is 200 words; Essay 2 is 200 words and Essay 3 is 600 words. My test takers often struggle in trying to figure out how to scale down their writing into a tight well written essay.

When you write lesson plans many of you are used to using a "template" and so if a friend of yours had a great lesson idea and you decided to use it as well, your lesson plan probably looked very similar to theirs. This is because you are trained to use templates on your lesson plans. When you do this on the test it sounds plagiarized or copied. And then you fail because it doesn't sound like original writing. *(This is why it is important not to work with a friend when you are taking these tests.)*

When you wrote term papers for school you were usually writing something about a pedagogical theory or a prominent person in the field of education. You didn't write papers criticizing Piaget for his theories or arguing why Bloom's

Taxonomy was outdated, or why Vygotsky misunderstood the big picture in education.

In term papers you were basically asked to write exposition: explaining something. Your papers were basically proof to the instructor that you read the assignment and understood it. That is why most test takers do not have a problem with the first essay. It's asking you to do the exact same thing. The first essay is the easiest one to master.

Essay 1

Essay 1 is asking you to, in 200 words, summarize what each side has said and evaluate the strength of their arguments.

Essay 1: From the NYSTCE Preparation Guide:

Use the passages to respond as follows.

In a response of approximately 100–200 words, identify which author presents a more compelling argument. Your response must:

- outline the specific claims made in each passage;
- evaluate the validity, relevance, and sufficiency of evidence used to support each claim; and
- include examples from both passages to support your evaluation.

Summarize Passage A and Passage B and then objectively state who makes the better argument. This is not about who you agree with. It's about WHO WROTE THE BETTER PASSAGE? Your opinion is not the point here.

- Is the author's voice professional?
- Does the author cite reliable sources or just state opinion?
- Do the statements in the article make sense or are they exaggerations or equivocations?
- Is the idea clear and easy to understand?

Write the essay in three paragraphs.

- Paragraph 1 summarize Passage A
- Paragraph 2 summarize Passage B
- Paragraph 3 Mention both passages and say why one is better as it is written.

When writing this essay it is important that you convey a clear understanding of what the writer is trying to say about the topic. You also want to document the citations or evidence they use to back up their claim.

Common mistakes that test takers make:

- ***Debating the topic instead of just explaining the positions.***

Example: Summarizing passage A and then in the second paragraph writing something like this:

Although the author of Passage A makes some strong points about the use of car seats in cars, the Author of Passage B makes a better point. It's clear that there has been no real evidence to back up the claims that lack of car seat use is connected to fatalities in cars. My son stopped using the car seat when he was five and he's never been hurt. So I agree with passage B.

Wrong. This should be saved for Essay 3.

- ***Misunderstanding who said what.***

Sometimes when you are rushing you accidentally attribute an idea to the wrong writer. Take time to make a brief outline of who said what and who is on which side. Mixing up the names of the authors is a careless mistake that will cost you a lot of points. Pay attention to who is listed as Passage A and who is Passage B. Instead of referring to the passages this way, refer to them by the title and the last name of the author.

- *Not carefully citing.*

You should always write the name of the article and the author if possible. This will also help you to avoid mixing up Passage A and Passage B. Don't use those terms. Instead always write the name of the author and the title of the passage.

Please note the citations for these essays don't follow the MLA format

(Johnson, 324) (<<<NO!)

Instead you would write it out. Ex.

In John Smith's article entitled "Let's Pass the Test" he states.....

Once you mention the name of the author you can thereafter use just the last name. Ex.

Further, Smith contends that.....

- *Writing outside interpretation instead of just summarizing what the passages state.*

You are just writing about the passages and what they say. Nothing else.

In the Essay 3 you are supposed to bring in outside ideas but not in Essay 1 or Essay 2. These two essays should only discuss what you have read in the Passages. That's why they are so short.

Each essay is a brand new essay.

Please note that each one of the essays should "stand alone." In other words you have to start each one of your essays anew as if the evaluator has not read any of the other essays. Many times students assume that the essays are supposed to "build on each other." This is not true. Each essay is unique. They don't have to agree or build on each other. Let's look at an example of what that means.

Who wrote the better article doesn't mean "Who do you agree with?"

Say we are writing an essay evaluating two opinions about the experience of racism in education during the Civil Rights movement.

Passage A *is written by a member of the NAACP and shares an anecdotal story about his grandmother's experiences growing up in Mississippi.*

Passage B is written by a member of the KKK. He cites information from "The Bell Curve," "Brown versus the Board of Education of Topeka Kansas" and several studies done on the issues of integration in schools.

Who wrote the better article? Now, is there anyone who would agree with someone from the KKK? If you do you shouldn't be a teacher. Put down this book and go away. However, in assessing the Passage, if they wrote the better article then *they wrote the better article*. In **Essay 1** I might say that the writer wrote a better article. But in **Essay 3** I would totally disagree with him. These essays do not have to build on each other. They are each independent essays.

This is an extreme example but it clarifies what you will be expected to do on the test. Don't worry they will not ask you to evaluate articles by hate groups on the actual test!

Example:

In John Smith's article entitled "African American Experiences with Racism in Education," the author explains his grandmother's experiences going to school in Mississippi during the Civil Rights era. He shares anecdotal stories about her perspective and the challenges she faced in trying to get a fair and equal education. Smith explains that her difficulties informed the way she viewed education and the way she encouraged her own children in school.

In Tom McNasty's article, "Segregated School Systems Work Best" he explains that statistics show a marked difference in the way African American students perform in school compared to other ethnic groups. He cites information from "The Bell Curve" and "Study X" that indicate these disparities have a severe impact on the overall effectiveness of school systems. McNasty's position is that segregated school systems work better over-all.

Both authors make compelling points, however John Smith's article has a narrow focus that examines only one woman's anecdotal experience. Smith uses diary entries and quotes from interviews to substantiate his position. On the other hand McNasty's article includes citations from reputable sources and studies to back up his claims. He evaluates several different studies in his argument and thus makes a stronger point.

Now look at the above essay and see that it is 200 words. You'll have more information once you see the actual Passages that will help you get to your word count of 200. *(note: you should always write to the highest end of the word count range they ask of you)* As you can see it's a very simple and straightforward essay. ***It is not about who you agree with.***

Essay 2

From the NYSTCE Preparation Guide:

"Use a single passage and the chart to respond to the following assignment.

In a response of approximately 100–200 words, explain how the information presented in the charts can be integrated with the author's central argument about the topic in either Passage B OR Passage A. Your response must:

- explain how specific information presented in the charts either supports or counters the author's claims, reasoning, and evidence; and
- include examples from the passage and the charts to support your explanation."

Essay 2 is an analysis of the chart. Please keep in mind that the chart is CORRECT. Do not make the mistake of confusing the accuracy of the chart with the accuracy of the statements made in the Passages. The prompt will ask you to analyze the chart and evaluate whether or not the chart backs up the statements made in one passage.

- **Paragraph 1:** Summarize the points made in the passage that are relevant to the chart. Use the name of the article and the author. Use a quote or paraphrase what was said. Explain what the author means.
- **Paragraph 2:** Use the title of the chart and quote specific details. Explain how it supports or does not support the statement made in the passage. EITHER passage A or Passage B. Remember it will ONLY be one.

Common mistakes that students make:

- Panicking over the chart and making it harder than it actually is.
- Extending the data in the chart beyond the numbers that are there.
- Misreading the prompt.

Understanding the Prompt

Be mindful to carefully read the prompt. Many of my students mistakenly think they are being asked this question:

Does Passage A back up the information in the chart? (This is wrong, you are not being asked this question. This is backwards!)

You are being asked this:

Does the **chart** back up the statements made in the **passage**?

Be careful here. Sometimes they change the way they word the prompt. I had one student last year who had prepped to take a position. When she saw the chart she interpreted it and charged ahead writing how it "did not support" the argument made in Passage B. She did this because she misunderstood the prompt She thought that prompt said "Does the chart back up Passage B?" and so she wrote that it did not back up passage B. But her friends who took the test at the same time all realized that the prompt actually said, "Does the chart back up Passage A?" They all wrote that the chart did back up Passage A. She wrote the opposite by mistake. She failed the test by 1 point.

How annoying! Make sure you understand exactly what the prompt is asking you.

There are two different types of prompts:

Does the chart back up the statements made in Passage A or Passage B?

(This is an either/or question. You would need to figure out which passage the chart backs up and explain why it backs it up. In other words, "which one *does* it back up.")

or

Does the chart back up Passage A? or

Does the chart back up Passage B?

(You will be asked one or the other and this is a **yes or no** question. If it does back it up you would need to explain why. If it **doesn't** back it up then you would need to explain why.)

Make sure you understand which prompt you are being asked. I think a lot of students who fail the test by a few points have mistakenly answered the wrong prompt. Be careful.

Now let's move on to the types of charts you might see on the test. Keep in mind I cannot tell you about the exact type of chart so I am using ones that are *similar* but *different*. Don't just read this study guide and then go down assuming the charts say the same thing that you read here. They will be different.

Understanding the Charts & Essay 2

Many of the students in my class are completely intimidated by the idea of interpreting a chart. This is because they are over-thinking what they are being expected to do. I myself had the same problem when I first began teaching the test. I looked at some charts and sat there completely confused. So I went to a friend of mine who had studied statistics. I discussed the charts we were using with him and then gave him the charts and said "I'll pay you 100 dollars per chart if you can help me understand how to clearly explain it."

Then I went back several days later and he handed me back the charts and told me I was being ridiculous and not to pay him. I had already talked to him about the charts and it was clear to him that I basically understood them. I had thought that my understanding was too simple and there *must* be more to it. He asked me an important question that I want you to consider: "Why do people **make** charts?" People make charts to *simplify* a lot of written data into an easy to read format. There is really nothing more that you need to know about a chart. All the information you need is right on the chart. There is no "hidden meaning" beyond what you yourself put into the chart in your fear that you don't understand it. Again, this is caused by over-thinking; stop over-thinking it!

Do you honestly believe that the test makers have asked you to do a deep analysis of a complicated chart in 200 words? Think about it for a second. Your second essay is only about 200 words and in that word allotment you are also expected to explain one of the passages. They are not asking you to put on your genius level thinking here; they are simply asking you to summarize it in a clear way in about 100 words. *(To help you understand how short that is, this paragraph is 100 words. It's not very long is it?)*

Once you understand the chart and how to explain it, then you can also use it as back-up evidence in your third essay. In other words you'll explain how the chart backs up your argument. That would be about a two sentence explanation. So keep in mind that the best way to handle a chart is to keep it simple. Remember that old adage: KISS---keep it simple silly!

Points to remember

- Always read the title and subtitles on the chart to understand what the data is about.
- Look for matching trends if comparing information in several small charts.
- Read the "key" if the chart has different symbols
- Read dates: if they are given, they are important. You should always refer to the date if it is given.
- Not everything on the chart is relevant. When looking at expenditure charts sometimes they put subtotals across. You really only need to look at the last line if they are adding and/or subtracting figures.
- The charts are not always related to the specific Passages. They are asking you to see how the information in the chart "can be integrated" into the Passage's argument. Don't just assume it's about the exact same information.

Data is just Data

The other important thing my friend told me is this: Charts are collection of data and data doesn't prove anything. Data is just data. It's the interpretation of the data that is either correct or incorrect. The question you are being asked in Essay 2 is if the statements made in either Passage A or Passage B are backed up by the data in the chart. They are asking you to explain who is manipulating the data to make a point. This is something that happens all the time in Media. They are asking you to catch when a writer is basically *lying* by pretending the data means something it doesn't, or to verify when a writer is correct in their interpretation. ***(Please note, you should never accuse the writer of lying. It's tacky.)***

Consider in your own life how many times you've watched some "expert" on the news talk about a "scientific study" that "proves" something. Remember when years ago we were told that eating fat was detrimental to our health? So people ran off and started diets that "cut out all fat!" Then years later we hear of another "supposed expert" who said, "Wait, no! We actually realized that fat is good! It's the carbohydrates that are causing you to gain weight!" So people ran out and started doing the Atkins diet and ate lots of fat and vegetables. Then someone else came along and said "No wait…." You get the picture. Data doesn't prove anything. Data is just data. What you are being asked to do is to see if the data backs up what the person says it means.

Let's look at an example that I use in my class. The topic is "Should we spend more money on technology in schools?"

The Data: 59% of all public schools have computers in the classroom.

Passage A: The Mayor: *"The majority of all schools have computers in the classroom."*

Passage B: The UFT Rep: *"Half of all schools do not have computers in the classroom."*

If you look at the statements made and consider the data can you see how, in a way, both statements are sort of backed up by the data? But can you also see how both of them are making manipulated statements?

There are basically three considerations needed in evaluating the validity of the statement: I call these **The Three Flaws!**

A. **Bias**

Do you see how the Mayor would probably want to interpret the data one way? Why? Well, probably because he doesn't want to spend more money in schools. He also wants to look like this wonderful mayor who is doing a great job. Look how successful he's been! The majority of schools have computers.

Do you see how the UFT rep is biased as well? She is probably on the side of the teachers and is pushing for more funding in the classroom. So right off the bat we have wonder if she is being sincere.

B. **Exaggeration**

The mayor says "the majority" and if we think about it, technically 59% is a majority. But he's kind of exaggerating the meaning here. Most people, when hearing the phrase "the majority" would think it meant 80-90% not 59%, right? If you didn't actually see the data, how would you interpret what he said? This is an example of a manipulation.

Likewise, the UFT rep is exaggerating as well. She writes that "Half" the schools don't have computers. Well if 59% do have computers, then 41% don't have computers. 41% is not "half;" that would be 50%. Can you see how she's exaggerating here?

C. **Equivocation**

This is a tricky one. Think about what the word sounds like it means. It sounds like it means "equal." But that's not what equivocation means. Equivocation means making something *sound like it is the same thing*, when it is **not** the same thing.

Most teachers have a hard time catching this. So let's take a second a look at the data and statements again. See if you can catch it.

The Data: 59% of all public schools have computers in the classroom.

Passage A: The Mayor: *"The majority of all schools have computers in the classroom."*

Passage B: The UFT Rep: *"Half of all schools do not have computers in the classroom."*

Can you see where they are trying to make two different things look like the same thing? Look below to see where I've underlined two different wordings.

The Data: 59% of <u>all public schools</u> have computers in the classroom.

Passage A: The Mayor: *"The majority of <u>all schools</u> have computers in the classroom."*

Passage B: The UFT Rep: *"Half of <u>all schools</u> do not have computers in the classroom."*

What is the difference between "all public schools" and "all schools"?

All schools could include private and charter schools. Do taxpayers pay for the computers in a private school? Who pays for the technology in private schools? The parents do through the tuition fees. So how can we include these schools in the statements if they don't apply to what the chart is talking about? Do you see this is a manipulation that can skew the numbers?

Another Example: Let's look at another example. "Should parents be required to use car seats for children in their cars while driving?

At this point, I'm not even going to put the chart here. Just the TITLE of the chart. Always read the title of the chart.

Data: Accident injuries related to lack of using a child car seat while driving.

Passage A: Johnny Doe: Requiring Children to Use Car Seats is Unnecessary and Dangerous

As a person who grew up in the 70's before car seats became mandatory, I remember sitting in the back seat of a car with my brothers and passing toys back and forth. I grew up in a large family of 5 and we generally wore seat belts and were fine. I don't ever remember hearing of a family that had a child die from being in a car accident because they were sitting in the back seat of a car. I also remember riding my bicycle without a helmet or knee pads and no one ever died from crashing their bicycle. Today it seems that the public has been duped into believing that children are at the risk of dying from some terrible injury if they are not protected constantly. Even playgrounds are made with padded foam in case a child should fall off the monkey bars. It has gotten to the point of being crazy. There is no evidence that using car seats will prevent fatalities. In fact the opposite is true. When air bags were first introduced in cars, many children were killed because they were forced to be in car seats and when placed in the front seat, as the airbag went off when a parent suddenly braked, the child suffered horrible head injuries and died. Then parents were told to put the car seats in the back of the car. Recent headlines are filled with horrifying stories of children trapped in car seats who died from heat exposure when parents forgot them and they couldn't get out of the car seat. Mandatory car seat laws are causing much more harm than good. Evidence shows that there is no reduction in the amount of fatalities that occurred in accidents when children were in car seats.

Now when you read this, there may be parts of the argument that you can agree with, ex: *over protective policies; the dangers related to the use of car seats.* But overall, your reaction to this article would probably be, "What the heck is this person talking about? The data is about injuries in accidents, not just fatalities."

It is very important to always read the titles of the charts to understand exactly what the data means.

Let's deconstruct for THE THREE FLAWS

A. **Bias.** The writer is using examples from his own personal life experiences. This is a logical fallacy known as "anecdotal." Instead of using compelling evidence and data, he's basing his argument on his life as a kid. Just because he didn't "hear of anything" doesn't prove anything. Maybe his parents didn't want to scare him or his siblings so they never said anything. Please note that it's not always going to be obvious from the name of the author if they are biased. Sometimes you have to pick it up from their wording.

B. **Exaggeration.** Notice how the writer uses exaggerated language that can't possibly be true. *"No one ever died." "Mandatory car seat laws are causing much more harm than good."* He's giving examples without backing up any of the claims. He's exaggerating the examples of children who were killed by being left in a car as being some sort of "statistical representation." The actual numbers are small.

Here are the facts from the study entitled Heatstroke Deaths of Children in Vehicles:

Total number of U.S. heatstroke deaths of children left in cars, **1998-present: 661**

That's only a few victims a year, not some large percentage. It's tragic, but it isn't something that is representative of car seat use in general.

C. **Equivocation.** Car seats are not just used to prevent deaths. They are also used to prevent injuries. A child could be profoundly injured in a car accident but not actually die. Consider a child who becomes paralyzed because they injure their neck from whiplash. Consider children who suffer traumatic brain injuries because they hit their head on the seat in front of them. Consider the children who suffer from broken arms and legs or internal injuries. Consider the scars and facial injuries, blindness etc. All of these are tragic consequences from not using the car seat.

Go back and see how the writer only discusses fatalities and not injuries as well. Look at his wording "die" "died" "killed" "fatality" etc. Now what is the title of that chart again?

Data: Accident injuries related to lack of using a child car seat while driving.

Can you see how the writer is being manipulative and not actually discussing the data properly? This is a very common form of manipulation. We see it daily in news media stories. When a Presidential candidate is talking about "immigration issues" don't you notice how they avoid talking about the total picture and only focus on one point that backs up their claim? Keep an eye out for this when reading your articles.

Remember something important: these articles are just editorial OPINIONS of the writers. I bet some of you read this essay thinking "Who is this idiot? He's completely wrong." Good. That's the reaction you should have when reading any of the articles on any writing exam. These are just "some guy's opinion." Sometimes they will sound very logical and informed. That still doesn't make them an expert. The articles you read should be read with a skeptical eye because very often the writers use manipulations in their writing to try to sound more authoritative than they really are.

Types of Charts:

In this section I alternate between font sizes to make it easier to keep track of the different explanations. Please also note that all the data is entirely made up. The purpose of this section is to explain each type of chart not these ones specifically.

Pie charts

Pie Charts are used to show a breakdown of one type of variable in a group, population or category. They are generally very simple to understand. The key is to consider the topic of the category and the titles of the segments. For example, population break downs are often used on school websites to let people know the different types of ethnic groups that attend that school.

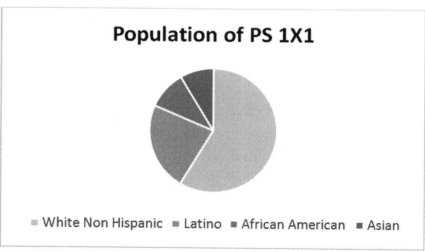

Line Charts

Line charts are used to track trends over a period of time. These types of charts are made to show a pattern of behavior, action, progression, increase or decrease. The title of the chart tells you the specific nature of the data. The numbers going up are measurements. The wording going across is usually a date. These types of charts are generally used to show a change in something over several years.

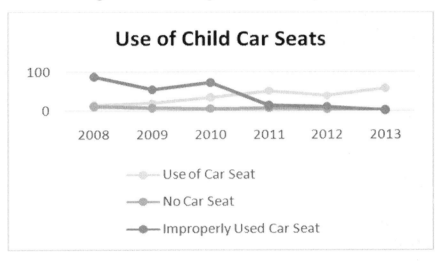

This type of chart will use several different variables and when you read it you can draw a conclusion. In the chart above we can see that from 2010 to 2013 there was a sharp drop in Improperly Used Car Seats. If we were to compare this chart to another chart that showed a drop in injuries to children in the same time period, we could logically conclude that there was a *correlation* between improperly used car seats and injuries.

Sales or Loss and Return on Investment

These types of charts are designed to tally money or funds so that you can see how much something may have cost over a period of time. These are very simple and easy to understand. The data comes from the total column. Remember, you're just being asked to summarize the data in the chart, not to explain every single detail. The key is to pay attention to the information relevant to the arguments being made in the passages. And to do basic addition and subtraction.

Projected Return on Investment vs. Tuition

	4-year Public University	4-Year Private College	For-Profit School
Tuition-Total 4 year cost	$80,000	$350,000	$95,000
Average Loan Amount	$14,500	$23,400	$37,000
Projected Lifetime earnings of Graduates with Bachelor's Degree	1,500,000	2,300,000	1,800,000
20 Year Net ROI	$564,000	$719,000	5325,000

The above chart would be used to consider the **ROI** or Return on Investment when going to a college. The *investment* is what you would spend on tuition, including loans. The *return on the investment* is how much money you expect to make in a salary because you have gotten your degree. When we look at the chart we can see that a 4 year degree at a private college might cost a lot more at first, but in the end it gives a much higher return on investment.

Consider your own experience as a teacher. Many times your tuition, application fees and cost of certification fees seem excessive. In fact when talking with many people about what I do for a living they are often shocked at how expensive it is to become a teacher. Consider just the

EdTPA submission costs alone. Now think about why you are willing to pay these costs? It is because you anticipate getting a good job, making a good salary with benefits and retirement. You will have gotten a "return" on your investment. So it is worth it to you. Would you be willing to do all this work to make $10 an hour? Probably not.

Returns on investments are not always about money alone. For example, if a parent pays for a Math tutor for their child in school to help them improve their grades, they are not anticipating an economic return on investment. Instead they are anticipating their child doing well on their Math tests. If they don't it is not a good return on their investment. *(This is one reason that BEC's motto is: "We stay with you until you pass!". We want to be a good return on your investment.)*

Avoiding safety hazards could also be a good return on investment. If a company buys goggles for all their employees and it reduces the number of eye injuries on the job, it is also a good return on investment.

When analyzing charts like this you want to consider the costs and the types of returns to be expected ie; economic, quality of education, improved productivity. Keep it as simple as possible.

Voting List Charts

These charts often confuse people because they don't "look like charts." Most test takers are expecting to see numbers or lines or graphs when looking at charts. However, argumentative writing prompts will often pick a topic of controversy and then show you how the States in the U.S. voted for reforms or restrictions.

Let's take the topic **Gun Law Limitations in the US**

Keep in mind, that despite all the arguing and ranting you see in the news, The Right to Bear Arms is a Constitutional Right. It is very unlikely that this right will ever be taken out of the Bill of Rights. Why? Well the Bill of Rights are considered "sacrosanct" in the U.S. When something is a Constitutional Right it is a very different thing than other laws.

Sacrosanct means that it's essentially "untouchable." If you start messing around with the 2nd Amendment, what's to stop the Government from saying *"Hey these Bill of Rights aren't so sacred any more are they? Let's start changing the other ones as well. Who needs freedom of speech? People cause a lot of trouble with hate speech, let's change that one too."*

Can you see this ever happening? Not likely. So how does the US deal with a controversial issue like the right to bear arms? Instead of arguing over that right, they argue over how *the law interprets that right.* How do certain states define the right to bear arms? Some states interpret the law to mean the right to have weapons for personal safety and hunting. So those states would DEFINE the right to bear arms in a restrictive definition.

Other states would define the right to bear arms as a Constitutional Right to defend oneself against a government take-over. They would DEFINE the right to bear arms to include assault weapons and machine guns. Some states would define the right to bear arms as "we can have whatever we want." So these are places that would sell guns out of Walmart because some people use them for recreational activities and hobby collections.

Definition	Voting States
Security	NY, NJ, DL, FL, OH, MD, KS, WY, CA, NM, ID, ND, SD, NC, SC, WV, VA, CO, KY
Hunting	VT, NY, FL, WY, NM, TN, TX, CA, NV, KS, IL,
Federal	TX, TN, AZ, NM, UT,
Recreational	TX, TN, AZ, NM, UT, ND, SD
Security	Restrictions to the definition only to be used as a form of personal security and includes hand guns and shot guns.
Hunting	Restrictions to the definition include weapons that have been clearly designed for hunting and sportsmanship.
Federal	Restrictions to the definition are unlimited and allow private citizens to purchase and use any weapon that is manufactured and sold legally in the US.
Recreational	Restrictions to the definition are unlimited and allow private citizens to purchase and use any weapon that is manufactured and sold legally in the US at gun ranges for shooting practice, hobbies and recreation.

Voting List Charts would look something like this: (please note, for the purposes of this book, I'll just make up the data. This way it's completely original. The data is representative not real)

Restrictions to the Definitions of the Right to Bear Arms

Voting List Charts are telling you how states voted for restrictions or how they voted for the definition of the law.

There are several ways to interpret the chart but the easiest way is to see if there is a majority of states that voted one way and a minority of states that voted another.

Example

According to the chart entitled "Restrictions to the Definitions of the Right to Bear Arms," the majority of the states voted for the definition of the 2nd Amendment to mean that people can own guns for security purposes. This definition limits the interpretation of the law to mean only handguns and shotguns may be owned.

The key to understanding these charts is to read the definitions below the list of voting states to see what they were voting about.

Financial trends in areas

When looking at a chart that describes financial trends, the most important thing to look for is a drastic "increase" or "decrease." Sometimes people don't understand that stability is an indication that something is working just fine and there's no need to fix it. Let's look at an example related to the debate of whether or not NYC should privatize parking meters.

Parking meter use and revenue in NYC

U stands for Users (by millions)

R stands for Revenue (millions made)

(please note, for the purposes of this book, I'll just make up the data. This way it's completely original. The data is representative not real)

Parking meter use and revenue in NYC

Borough	2007	2008	2009
Queens	(U) 2,651 (R) 5,346	(U) 2,472 (R) 5,201	(U) 2,772 (R) 5,822
Brooklyn	(U) 3,656 (R) 7,012	(U) 3,472 (R) 6,591	(U) 3,972 (R) 6,834
Staten Island	(U) 2,675 (R) 4,341	(U) 2,809 (R) 4,408	(U) 2,972 (R) 4,634
Manhattan	(U) 7,634 (R) 9,941	(U) 7,113 (R) 9,421	(U) 7,472 (R) 9,745
Bronx	(U) 4,608, (R) 6,575	(U) 4,333 (R) 6,208	(U) 3,986 (R) 6,034

What do we see when we look at this chart? First we read it across for each Borough to see if there are changes in the amount of users and revenue from year to year. What we see is that the numbers fluctuate up and down but for the most part we are not seeing a drastic problem. In other words we're not seeing a huge decrease in the amount of money made. Although the revenue goes up and down, in general it stays in the same range. When I've used this example in class most students were confused because they expected to see a matching trend overall, but there isn't one. For example the Users and Revenue go UP for Queens by 2009. But the Users and Revenue go DOWN for the Bronx. Many students couldn't understand how to interpret it.

This chart would be associated with the topic of NYC's considering privatizing parking meters throughout the city.

What does **privatization** mean? Basically it means that the city has decided that instead of the city using part of its budget for managing the parking meters and parking lots throughout the city, they will sell or lease the ***management contract*** to a private company. That company is then responsible for cleaning up the parking lots, repairing the meters if they break, hiring maintenance employees and collecting the money from the meters on a regular basis.

Why would the city want to do this? Well consider how much money we would save as taxpayers if we sold or leased the contract to a private company who would then hire their own employees. The city would no longer have to hire employees to do this job. Although the city would maintain a supervisory role in this contract, the monies made from the meters would go to the private company. The company would use that money to manage all the parking meters in the city.

Another consideration is whether the city is making a lot of money from parking meters just the way it is right now. Do we consider millions of dollars, worth it? How expensive is it to hire all these parking meter employees? City workers tend to have good medical coverage and retirement plans. City employees tend to have good job security and are given raises based on years of employment. Even though the employee may have started off at minimum wage, they could be making $30 an hour after several years. Are we making enough money off the meters to pay for all of that? Or is the city just breaking even? Would it be smarter to have someone else take care of it and use that money for something else?

When you see a chart that is comparing financial trends in specific areas, the key to understanding the chart is to keep each line specific to the area and to then figure out overall if the numbers are going up or down and ask yourself, how drastic is that increase or decrease? And to also examine how much money we are making compared to how much it costs for the city to pay for it out of its budget.

Privatization issues also show up on federal levels and it's the same type of consideration. Is it better for the federal government to take care of it themselves or to sell or lease the contract to a private company? Think about how much more a federal employee would make in salary, benefits and retirement compared to a part-time minimum wage employee of the private company?

The issue of privatization of parking meters in NYC was decided against for a number of reasons. Parking meters generate a revenue stream for the city. The danger of selling or leasing a management contract is that once a private company has taken over, they have the right to do what they want within reason. One thing they could do is to raise the cost of the parking. How would that impact the people who live in the city if parking meters became more expensive? Would it create a divide between the rich and the poor where only the rich could afford to pay for parking at meters?

Another way we could examine the chart would be to look for a rough estimate of how much money each person paid for their parking. So for example if roughly **7 million** people paid around *10 million dollars* for parking, then the average person paid *about $1.50* each time they used it. This number gives us an idea if the pricing is fair. Think about how much you would consider a fair price for paying for parking each time. A rich person might be willing to pay $45 to park in a parking garage for the same amount of time. If they are the ones who get the right to control the prices, they would probably want to make more money. Parking in NYC is a major issue for most people. Privatizing parking meters could create more problems than it solves.

The other problem is that there is the possibility of bribery to get the contract. Chicago had a huge problem when it was revealed the kickbacks and bribery were used to try to influence the government to give it to a specific company. The idea that something so essential to people who live in a city could be turned over to greedy people who wanted to twist it into an expensive and unfair cost was very problematic.

Ultimately the decision was made in NYC that the revenue made from parking offset the cost of maintaining them with city employees and that it was better to manage it from within.

Causation versus Correlation Charts

You may have heard these terms when people have discussed whether or not vaccinations are causing Autism. There are many parents out there who insist that their child was perfectly healthy until they got their childhood vaccinations. Most doctors insist that there is no evidence to back up this claim. The debate has gone on for decades.

What does causation mean? It basically means cause and effect. One thing led to another. So in this argument the parents are saying that the vaccine caused Autism.

What does correlation mean? Correlation means that we see a pattern connected to one thing but it's not necessarily true that thing one thing **caused** the other to happen. For example some may argue that parents who brought their children home from a doctor's visit and watched the child closely suddenly began to notice things in the child they didn't before. Or it could just be a coincidence. We can't say it caused it.

Many times topics for argumentative essays are chosen for their debate about correlation versus causation. One side usually puts forth theories and data that they *say* proves that: X causes Y. The other side will argue that you can't really be *sure* that X causes Y because there are many other variables at play. One way to avoid making a mistake in your interpretation of these arguments is to completely remove the words "cause" "causation" "caused" from your mind when considering the evidence.

For example I would not be wrong if I said that "there is a correlation between autism diagnoses and vaccinations." But I would be wrong if said that getting a vaccination causes autism.

When evaluating the evidence related to these types of debates you'll want to consider the "limits of the study." That means ages, dates and types of studies done. You also want to consider other possible reasons or "variables" that could be influencing the data. For example in the previous debate that "use of car seats prevents injuries" the person who wrote the opposing point stated that using car seats was causing more deaths because parents were forgetting their children in the back seat.

Is that causation? Or is that correlation? What other variables may have caused this sudden increase in children left in cars? One reason is that more and more people are using cell phones. So instead of staying focused on the road people are not paying attention. In most of the cases involving children left in cars, the parents had taken a call or texted someone right before they got out of the car and forgot their child. It was the distracted mind that caused the problem, not the car seat.

Another example is the idea that "smoking causes lung cancer." Most of us would consider this to be common sense understanding. What's interesting is that in reality less than 10% of people who smoke actually get lung cancer. Many people would assume that the number would be much higher.

We can't really say that, smoking causes cancer because if it did, then almost everyone would get cancer. At the same time it would be pretty stupid to ignore the *correlation* between cancer, heart disease, emphysema and other health issues as they are related to smoking. When looking at charts that compare one action to a consequence, be sure to talk about *correlation* instead of *causation* and you will avoid this pitfall.

Comparative Charts

When comparing two charts we want to look for matching trends that show a correlation between two variables.

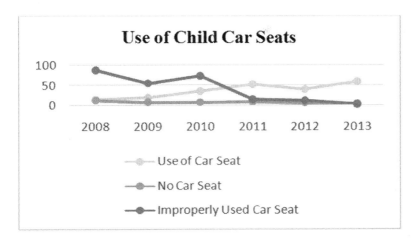

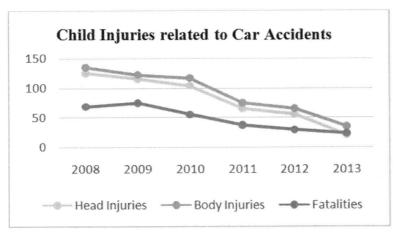

When we compare these two charts we can see a correlation between the reduction in the number of improperly used car seats and a reduction in the number of injuries from accidents.

Understanding Percentage vs. Total Money Spent.

This type of data is actually very simple but people tend to overthink it. Remember when I told you to stop doing that? Stop doing that.

Let's look at example related to salary and rent.

It's 2010 and Tracy Jackson is a teacher who makes $24,000 a year. She has an apartment for which she pays $1,000 a month which is $12,000 a year. How much of a percentage of her total income is she spending on rent? She's spending 50% of her total income on rent.

$24,000 total income

$12,000 rent per year is 50% of her total income.

Now in 2015 she gets certified and she gets a job making $100,000 a year. She decides to rent a nicer apartment. The apartment costs $2000 a month which is $24,000 a year. How much of a percentage of her total income is she spending on rent? She's spending 24% of her total income on rent.

$100,000 total income

$24,000 rent per year is 24% of her total income.

What's interesting here is that even though she's paying more money in rent, it's a smaller ***percentage*** of her overall budget. When evaluating an expenditure like this we need to keep two separate ideas in mind.

How much is she spending?

How much of a percentage of her budget is it?

Even though she's spending more money, she's spending **less** of a percentage of her over-all budget. So financially, it's a good economic decision.

If you read this and you don't understand it easily, please ask a friend to go over it with you. It's a very simple concept but sometimes people over-think it and confuse themselves.

This is generally something related to how much money the US Government is spending on something compared to what they did years ago. So for example, if we consider the Trans Alaska Pipeline project that was started in 1974-1977, the US government was probably spending less money on the research. **(and again remember I always make up the data in this book to make sure it's original. It is representative not real)**

Let's say between 1974 and 1977 the US spent *10 billion* dollars a year for this research. But back then the Gross Domestic Product (GDP) was *100 billion* dollars. Then it would have been 10 percent of our GDP.

Now the world is improving technologies, research is safer, they are using robots and machines to dig into the ground so it's cheaper as well. But we are spending *200 billion dollars* on the research project. However, today's GDP is *16 trillion dollars*. Even though we are spending *more money*, we are spending *less of a percentage* of our GDP.

The following example might seem silly but if you think about the Austin Powers movies, when Dr. Evil keeps going back and forth in time, he can't quite figure out how much ransom money he should demand. So for example, in 1997 he threatens to blow up the planet if we don't pay him 1 million dollars. He says this in a very dramatic way and everyone laughs at him because it's such a small amount in that era. Another time he goes back in time to 1969 and turns around and asks for 100 billion dollars. And everyone laughs at him as well because it's such a ridiculously large amount of money for that era.

The time period in which a budget was created will be based on how much money the country was able to produce, our GDP.

Essay 3: The Argumentative Essay

In Essay 3 you must take a position and either agree or disagree with the issue being debated. You must CONVINCE the reader that **you** are correct. The most common mistake I see in this essay is that writers are writing EXPOSITION instead of argumentative writing.

The instructions for writing the essay, based on the NYSTCE Preparation Guide are as follows:

"In an essay in your own words of approximately 400–600 words, present a fully developed argument that introduces and supports a claim assessing the benefits and risks of: TOPIC

- include a knowledgeable claim that demonstrates an understanding of the topic;
- use valid reasoning that draws on and extends the arguments in the sources provided;
- support **your** claim with relevant and sufficient evidence from all three sources; and
- anticipate and address at least one counterclaim."

Your essay should be written for an audience of educated adults. You must maintain an appropriate style and tone and use clear and precise language throughout. With the exception of appropriately identified quotations and paraphrases from the sources provided, your writing must be your own. The final version of your essay should conform to the conventions of edited American English. 400-600 words"

Five Paragraph Essay

- Paragraph 1 Introduction with a Thesis statement.
- Paragraph 2 First point to be addressed with examples (Make this the more logical example) and citation
- Paragraph 3 Second point to be addressed with examples and citation
- Paragraph 4 Counterclaim with citation from one passage and citation from the chart
- Paragraph 5 Conclusion

Which Side Should I Take?

This seems to be the number one confusion that most people have on the Essay 3 section of the test. Remember before when I told you that the articles are editorials? I said they are just "some guy's opinion." There is a tendency for test takers to defer to the authority of the Passages. They read the articles and then feel that they should agree with the person who wrote the better article. But what about the Passage written by the KKK guy? Would you want to write an essay agreeing with him just because you think he wrote the better article? It doesn't make any sense. The side that you should take and are expected to take is YOUR OWN. You are not being asked to parrot back someone else's ideas, you are supposed to be writing **your own opinion** on the topic.

Let's take a look at an example that I use in the class:

The Ferguson Riots: *(If you are unfamiliar with the story surrounding the Ferguson Riots, please take time to look it* *up on Wikipedia.)* Basically what happened in the Ferguson Riots is that a black teenager named Michael Brown got into an altercation with a police officer. The police officer then got out of his vehicle and went after Michael Brown, shooting him and killing him. The officer's justification for going after Michael Brown was that he matched the description of a perpetrator of a crime. Michael Brown had just left a store where he had stolen cigars. When the officer wasn't prosecuted the neighborhood started to riot. The Media exploded with commentary. Below I will write two statements that stood out to me:

The police officer murdered Michael Brown.

Michael Brown was a criminal that strong armed robbed a store.

These are bold statements. However in reading both these statements I don't agree with either of them. I'll deconstruct each one below.

The police officer <u>murdered</u> Michael Brown.

I don't agree with this statement. Murder has a specific legal definition and I don't think the officer murdered him. (You might, but I don't). I think the police officer "shot" and "killed" him but I don't think he murdered him. I also think that the police officer panicked and overreacted. I think that racism definitely had something to do with it as a big picture reason. I think that if you are police officer you shouldn't be racist and you definitely shouldn't be panicking and killing people because you can't handle the job. But this statement is too simplistic to me. I don't agree with it.

I would say this

The police officer shot and killed Michael Brown.

Now let's look at the other statement.

Michael Brown was a criminal that <u>strong armed robbed</u> a store.

I don't agree with this statement either. I've seen the video clip of Michael Brown in the store and I don't interpret it this way.

The first thing I take issue with is the statement that he "strong arm robbed a store." In my opinion this is a biased statement. What do we normally call it if someone goes into a store and steals something? We call it shoplifting. However, legally the situation can turn into a felony if you hurt an employee in the act. If you are "resisting apprehension" and you push someone who falls and is injured, it has now become a felony.

The interpretation of what happened was shifted because this "brawny young man" pushed past the employee. I don't think Michael Brown was resisting apprehension, I think he just responded to being bumped by the employee. I think the fact that he was so large and muscular overshadowed the fact that he was a teenager. You might not agree with me. The law doesn't agree with me, but I think that the statement would sound very different if I had to interpret it.

Michael Brown was a criminal that strong armed robbed a store.

becomes:

Michael Brown was a brawny teenager who shoplifted cigars and pushed past the store employee on the way out the door.

That's an entirely different sounding argument isn't it? So take a second to think about it. Which side should I agree with? I don't agree with either of them do I? I'm somewhere right in the middle. **Your opinion** is likely to be the same way when you write your essay. You might 100% agree with one side but you still have to write it from your own perspective. They don't want you to acknowledge the statements in the Passages as correct, they want you to <u>*use them*</u> to back up your **own** claim.

The most important questions I need to ask myself is what statement I'm going to make and which Passage is likely to have citations that I can use to back up my claim?

Here is my statement:

The incident that was the trigger for the Ferguson Riots was one in which a brawny, black teenager named Michael Brown, shoplifted cigars from a store. He then had an altercation with a police officer that soon escalated out of control resulting in Brown being shot and killed. These types of incidents are far too common in our country and we need to take a look at how racism plays a role in the relationships between police officers and young black men.

I would imagine that in writing my essay, using the rest of the Passage of the writer who made the first statement would be more useful to me in backing up my claims. But it's **not** about me AGREEING with that Passage. It's about me arguing my point and using the article as a <u>source for citations</u>. If you understand this distinction you are well on your way to writing a good essay.

Deconstructing the Essay by Paragraph.

As we developed our workshops we tried to create a rubric system that would help guide the writer by making sure they hit all the requirements needed to pass. We created an *original* rubric that was designed around the problems that most people seem to have in writing a timed exam off the top of their head. *(You can find the rubric at the end of the section on Essays)* However, this is not the only way to write an Argumentative Essay.

You may find other versions elsewhere, or you may think, "This is too simplistic, I write in a more sophisticated way." That's fine. There are as many ways to write an essay as there are writers. However, there are key grading points that have to be covered in order to get a passing score. We're not trying to get you a perfect essay. We're just trying to get you to pass. These tests are hard and when you are limited by time it is important to hit all the key grading points. Our rubric is designed to help you stay focused and organized which really is the most important skill needed on these types of essays.

We encourage you to start off writing using the rubric as you practice and then once you've mastered the steps, you can try to improve on your own. Remember! This is not a term paper. You don't have time or room in your word count for super flowery language or descriptions. The focus should be on making your point clearly understood and then backing it up properly. It is NOT about impressing them with your fabulous writing skills.

Viktor

I use Viktor as an example in the class to explain the importance of keeping it simple. Viktor was a Russian student of mine who is extremely intelligent. When he first spoke to me on the phone and told me he had already taken and failed the test, I was surprised. He is one of the smartest students I've ever had. I even gave him a discount for the class because I thought, *"He doesn't need me! He's brilliant!"* Even his email was written in a very sophisticated way. Imagine how shocked I was when he failed the test three times in a row *after* taking my class. 519, 511, 515. What?

I began to get very frustrated with him after he failed the second time because he wouldn't *listen to me*. I kept telling him that he was failing because he was so focused on writing these really long sophisticated sentences that used lots of "impressive" language but that didn't **clearly explain his point**. I started saying to him, "write it like you are explaining it to an 8th grader, not a PhD!' He wouldn't listen. He "refused to compromise" his writing style. Finally I got mad at him and told him this. *"Go in and do it the way I'm telling you the next time, and if you don't pass I'll pay for you to take it again. TRUST ME!"*

Guess what he got when he wrote it like he was explaining it to an 8th grade student? **A 567**. Do not try to impress the evaluator with your writing. Clearly explain your point and back it up. Yes, you probably could get an extra point or two if you are Mr. Fancy Pants, but you will lose **more** points because of lack of clarity in your argument. KEEP IT SIMPLE.

The Essay Evaluators are <u>not</u> College Professors!

For some reason, test takers in my class have this idea that the people grading the essays are college professors or writing experts. They are not!

If you google: "Who grades for Pearson" you will find a lot of articles that criticize the hiring practices of Pearson. For example one by the Washington Post points out that Pearson ran a Craigslist ad that offered $12 an hour and required a Bachelor's degree in *any field*.

One parent wrote an editorial that explained she was offered a job without ever having spoken to anyone at Pearson, simply based on her online application. According to Jennifer White, they didn't even verify her credentials before offering her the job. You can find this article by googling *'Congratulations to me Pearson.'* She also points out that there are "incentives" for productivity. This means they are encouraged to read quickly. This is why your fancy wording can cause you problems. I'll give two examples below.

Example 1

Once I worked with an essay evaluator in another test prep company. He had a background in Nursing, not English. He called me up laughing about how stupid the student writing the essay was because her first sentence was "so ridiculous." This is what the student wrote:

The issue of whether or not we should continue to fund Physical Education programs in schools is a topical debate.

The evaluator pointed out that the girl didn't know what topical meant. He was crowing with laughter, *"Topical means you put it on top of your skin! Like an ointment! What a stupid mistake!"* When he said this to me, I was shocked. He had failed her essay by one point because he was so annoyed by **her** mistake.

But he was WRONG. He only knew the medical definition of the word "topical." Here are the definitions of the word topical:

top·i·cal

adjective

1. (of a subject) of immediate relevance, interest, or importance owing to its relation to current events.

2. MEDICINE

relating or applied directly to a part of the body.

Source: Merriam-Webster's dictionary.

Remember that we never get the essays back, we don't see the actual grade. We don't see what they took off points for, we only see the plus scores. We don't even know how they grade it. In this situation the test prep evaluator failed the essay because **he** didn't know the proper definition of the word.

Example 2

I myself have a pretty decent vocabulary and I recently was grading an essay that had this as a sentence:

While there may be ephemeral financial drawbacks, they are nothing permanent that cause irreparable damage to the economy.

As soon as I saw **"*ephemeral,*"** a red flag went up. I didn't really know what the word meant. I had to stop and google it to check. It means "short term" so the writer used it correctly.

But stop and think about what has happened: <u>I stopped reading.</u> (If I was being paid based on my productivity, I might not even bother to look up the word.) It interrupted the flow of writing. It gave me a something to think might be wrong. This has a negative impact on the reader. Any time they have to *stop to try to figure out what you mean,* it's a bad idea.

Now let's see what the sentence would sound like if she had kept it simple.

While there may be short term financial drawbacks, they are nothing permanent that cause irreparable damage to the economy.

It still conveys her point and it's easy to understand. This works better. The fancy wording made it harder to understand and could result in a misunderstanding. As it is written now it sounds clear and professional.

FIVE and FIVE strategy

I encourage my teachers to use a five and five strategy. That means five paragraphs and five sentences. Try to keep this as your core of writing. You can always add more to it but you should *never* have less.

If five sentence paragraphs average about 100 words, and you have five paragraphs, it sets your word count at 500 words. With a few extra sentences you are at 600.

Five Paragraph Essay

- Paragraph 1 Introduction with a Thesis statement.
- Paragraph 2 First point to be addressed with examples
- Paragraph 3 Second point to be addressed with examples
- Paragraph 4 Counterclaim
- Paragraph 5 Conclusion

Five Sentence Introduction

To me it's very simple. 1,2,3,4,5. but I cannot tell you the number of times we've gone over this in class and people send me three sentence introductions with NO THESIS. Or they start debating in the introduction. THE INTRODUCTION INTRODUCES THE DEBATE it doesn't debate it yet.

Five sentences in the Introduction:

- Sentence 1 TOPIC SENTENCE
- Sentence 2 Proponents say; Those in favor state; Those who agree point out; etc. What does one side say *in general*, not in the Passages.

- Sentence 3 Those opposed say; Critics of this policy argue; Those who are against this idea point out, etc. What does one side say *in general*, not in the Passages.
- Sentence 4 Discuss why this is interesting or important in one sentence.
- **Sentence 5 THESIS**

Common Mistakes that Writers Make in the Introduction:

- **Not using a topic sentence:**

The writer should always start off the essay with a simple topic sentence that explains the issue being discussed in the passages. Writers should write the essay as if the person reading it has no idea at all what the topic is about. This is important because many students just get in the habit of "jumping right into it" because they have already written the first two essays. But appropriate argumentative writing has a topic sentence. Remember, each essay stands alone! Sometimes you might need two topic sentences to clearly explain the idea. That's ok. But you must explain the debate before you start writing.

A topic sentence introduces the topic of the *essay* to the reader.

Ex:

Recently in the United States there have been several mass shootings that have caused people to consider the definition of the Right to Bear Arms under the 2nd Amendment.

As more and more people in the United States are purchasing cars there has arisen a debate over whether or not it is practical to buy a used car versus a new car.

New York City has recently considered the use of privatization when dealing with the issues of managing parking lots and parking meters in the city.

With recent advancements in technology in the medical field, many hospitals are evaluating the use of robots in surgery instead of Doctors.

- **Arguing the topic instead of "Introducing the Debate"**

Writers often start off the introduction by arguing in the introduction. We need to save that for the **body** of the essay. But far too many writers will just start laying down evidence in the introduction. Don't use up all your points in the introduction. The point of the introduction is to "Introduce the Debate" not to "Debate the Topic."

- **Citing the Passages in the Introduction.**

The introduction is about the debate *in general*. We're not at the point yet of discussing the Passages. It is not necessarily *wrong* to cite the Passages in the introduction but when you do so you have a tendency to crowd out your ideas and make it difficult to read the introduction. In addition you are using up your citations in the introduction when you need them in the **body** of the essay. I always tell my students to never, ever, ever….mention the Passages in the introduction. Again, it's not necessarily wrong, but it always causes problems for test takers who are not very strong writers.

- **Not having a proper thesis statement**

Different types of writing use different types of thesis statements. An argumentative essay uses a specific type of thesis statement. If you don't have a proper thesis statement you can fail before you even begin.

Our evaluators will always look at the thesis statement first before beginning their evaluation and they will often decide that the essay is a "fail" if there is not a proper thesis statement. You can write a brilliant essay but if you don't have a proper thesis statement we will always score the essay with 2 pluses ++. Remember, you usually need 3 pluses +++ to pass. It is very important. I consider the thesis statement *the most important sentence* in the entire essay.

The thesis statement should follow these guidelines:

1. It should be the *last* sentence in the introduction
2. It should be a declarative statement not a personal opinion statement. (Do not write "In my opinion" "I believe" "I agree")
3. It should CLEARLY take a side in the argument
4. It should give **two reasons** for taking the side that will be discussed in the following paragraphs.

Wrong Examples: Take a look at these examples and see if you can see why they are wrong.

I believe that the Patriot Act is a good idea.

This is NOT a proper thesis statement.

Both authors make good points that we should consider.

This is NOT a proper thesis statement.

In this essay I plan to discuss the controversy surrounding the right to bear arms.

This is NOT a proper thesis statement.

The recent controversy surrounding the limits on Campaign Contributions causes us to consider the issues related to the long term impact on the economic issues that this policy will have on future election campaigns.

This is NOT a proper thesis statement. (Even though it sounds impressive, see how they only give one reason!)

Correct Examples:

Banning the use of cell phones in schools is a necessary policy because cell phones cause distractions and create liability issues.

The definitions of the Right to Bear Arms should be clarified because of safety issues and economic consequences.

Enforcement of the use of car seats in cars for children must be maintained for economic and safety reasons.

Do you see how these clearly take a side and give *two* reasons which will then be backed up in the essay? Think of your thesis statement as a CLUE to the reader letting them know what side you are on, and which *two* reasons you will then discuss in the rest of the essay.

Keep in mind you are giving a BRIEF reason, you are not explaining any of your reasoning in the introduction. You are just "setting up" the reader to understand what you will be writing. Have you ever read an essay and not been really sure what side the writer was on until later in the essay? A proper thesis statement avoids this mistake. Make sure that your next two paragraphs follow the same order of your reasons.

If your first reason is economic, then Paragraph 2 should be about your economic argument. If your second reason is about safety, then Paragraph 3 should be about safety. Make sure you make your arguments in the same order that you listed them in the thesis statement. If during editing you realize you mixed it up, just rewrite the thesis statement to match.

OUTLINE FOR ESSAY 3

Five paragraphs long, between 400-600 words (you should aim for around at least 550 if you want to pass)

- Paragraph 1 Introduction
- Paragraph 2 First point to consider, cite article and give an extra example
- Paragraph 3 Second point to consider, cite article and give an extra example
- Paragraph 4 Address the counterclaim and PROVE IT WRONG cite article and chart and give extra example
- Paragraph 5 conclusion

Understanding a "Strong" argument

This is another area, where being a teacher can sometimes narrow your thinking when writing an argument. Consider why most people go into teaching in the first place. I have never heard a teacher say *"I decided to become a teacher so I can make tons of money!"* Have you? Most teachers are drawn to teaching because it is a form of public service and they want to make a difference in the world.

Because of this, teachers tend to think with more of a "Social Awareness Mind" when considering ideas for an argument. Then when they write Essay 3 they start to notice that they are "repeating themselves" or using arguments that overlap. Has that ever happened to you? You feel like you are writing the same thing over and over again? A good way to avoid this is to separate your thinking into two categories. I refer to this in the class as the "Money Brain" and the "Social Brain" and point out you need an argument from ***both*** on the test.

What do I mean by using the "Money Brain" and "Social Brain?" One side tends to focus on money and the other side seems to focus on social responsibilities. It's like a yin and yang of good arguments. If you only use one side you are too extreme. Using both balances the essay and helps you to avoid sounding repetitive or narrow minded.

For example, although you may have been drawn to teaching because you wanted to make a difference in the world, you wouldn't do the job for free would you? The fact that you have a steady paycheck; that you have health insurance; that you are going to build a retirement are all part of your decision to become a teacher. Both sides helped you make your decision. Not just one. Take a look below at the list of different kinds of arguments for each side of thinking:

Money	Social
How much does it cost?	Health
Jobs, does it create jobs or create unemployment?	Safety
Taxes and Tax Payers	Personal freedoms and rights
Long term economic impact	Educational Issues
Big Picture	Environmental

When writing an outline for an essay, most people have been taught to jot down ideas in a pro or con list to try to figure out what side to take. In doing so you can have a tendency to overlook this balanced approach to arguments. You automatically give over "one side" of Money arguments entirely either to the "pro" or the "con" and so you miss ways to use it in your thinking.

Example: *Should I buy a used car instead of a new car?*

Pro	**Con**
Cheaper	Older car
Less Insurance	Less reliable

Do you see how we've made Money one side of the argument and other considerations the other side? This is wrong.

Instead we want to use the Money **and** the Social Responsibility arguments to set up frames of ideas and pick the one for which we have more "arguable" evidence. We want to consider the economic consequences for both sides of the issue, not just one side.

It's important to understand that when you are writing your essay you need to *sound like you are strongly arguing for one side*. But you don't necessarily have to actually personally agree with the side you are taking. They don't care what your REAL opinion is, but it must sound opinionated. They are looking at your ability to argue in a logical way and to make strong points. They honestly don't care which side you take, as long as you can back up your claims. This is important to keep in mind.

When we break it down into Money and Social ideas for each side of the argument it makes it easier to choose the side we are going to argue.

Pro Used Car

Money	Social
Cheaper	Convenience I can get it sooner
Less insurance costs	Environmental

Con Used Car

Money	Social
Cost of repairs would be unpredictable	Safety, used care is less reliable
A new car builds credit *Big picture argument.*	Environmental *Better gas mileage*

Now in reality you might *feel* something like this:

I don't care what the logic is behind getting a new car, I'm afraid I won't be able make the payments every month and I'd rather just buy a used car.

Or

I'm sick of driving a used car, I just want to get a new one that looks nice for a change!

See how these are not necessarily logical arguments? But they are how you *feel* and in real life you'd "go with your gut" or make a choice because of the way you feel about it.

That's not good enough in an essay. Being passionate is ***not*** the same thing as making a strong argument. You must be able to <u>back up</u> your claims. And you need **two** different claims. So you need to pick the side in the argument that you can ***write the best***. In this case we can see that there is a similar overlap between the Money argument and the Safety argument for the **Con Used Car** side. The first two are both about needing to repair the old car. So we might choose to argue the Pro Used Car side to avoid sounding like we are repeating ourselves in the essay.

Let's take a look at a mini essay using these arguments

Pro Used Car

Thesis:

Consumers should buy a used car whenever possible because it is more <u>economical</u> and <u>better for the environment.</u>

Notice in the thesis we take a side and give two reasons. The essay will then back up those two reasons in the same order.

Reason 1/ Paragraph 2: It is more economical

Reason 2/ Paragraph 3: It is better for the environment.

Now let's read:

As more and more people in the United States are purchasing cars, a debate has arisen over whether or not it is practical to buy a used car versus a new car.[1] When choosing the kind of car to buy, some people encourage consumers to buy a used car because insurance rates are cheaper.[2] Other economists suggest that it is less reliable to buy a used car and insist buying a new car is better.[3] It is an interesting discussion that has an impact on our roadways.[4] Consumers should buy a used car because it is more economical and better for the environment.[5]

For most consumers, the economic considerations in buying a car are part of the decision. Buying a new car is often much more expensive and requires the owner to purchase total coverage insurance. As John Smith points out in his article "Buying a Used Car Makes Sense," the cost of insurance rates for a new car are sometimes triple the cost than that of a used car. Added to the expense of monthly car payments, these costs can quickly put a consumer in debt if some life emergency like loss of a job were to arise. A used car is generally cheaper and in some cases able to be paid for outright which lowers insurance rates. Buying a used car is an economically sound decision.

Not only is buying a used car cheaper, it also has an impact on the environment. We live in times where people are quick to dispose of old items because a newer model comes out.

Junkyards are filled with cars, computers, appliances and outdated cell phones. Smith further explains in his article that "we owe it to future generations to be less willing to dispose of perfectly useable items while factories churn out more and more excess." Pollution from factories destroys the environment as well. Buying a used car is one way to be mindful of our environmental "footprint."

Tips to Remember!

Logical Arguments will generally look at the long term impact or "bigger picture"

- Economic Impact: Creating or losing jobs, Cost to tax payers
- Setting a legal precedent: Where do we draw the line?
- Violation of Civil Rights or Constitutional Rights. Is the government over stepping its bounds? Is this a violation of rights?
- Environmental issues: Will it hurt the environment in the long term? Will it create a hazard?

"Social arguments" will generally discuss things that relate to people's lives:

- Health Issues
- Social Responsibility
- Responsibility to future generations
- Safety Issues
- Educational Issues

Understanding Money Arguments

NOTE: This is a long and complex section so be sure that you give yourself time to read this section more than once. When you understand these ideas it becomes much easier to write an argumentative essay. This is the longest section in the book and I will break it up into categories to make it easier to read.

Money arguments can be tricky if you don't handle them properly, but there will *always* be a way to consider them in the essay and discussion.

The key to understanding Money Arguments is to think of the "big picture" and not just the individual. For example, I often use this topic in the class:

Should we ban smoking?

Now stop and consider what your first reaction to this topic would be. Most people think of "Health" reasons first and then they continue to repeat themselves in that line of thinking. Health is obviously a good argument to start with. However, when I ask teachers to consider how "Money" comes into the argument they haven't really thought of it before. Stop for a second and think about it.

In class, when I ask this question most people will say something like this: *"Well it's expensive to buy cigarettes so if a person stops smoking they will save money."* Is that what you were thinking now? If so, it's a typical type of response from a teacher. You are worried about individual needs and issues because, again, as a teacher you are trained to think of the students and their immediate needs. If you thought "bigger," *good for you,* you have the right kind of thinking going on.

You might be able to make an argument out of that point but the idea is too narrow and anecdotal. Anecdotal means "personal experiences" and they are usually biased. It's a small picture argument. Instead we want to think of "**big picture arguments**" and how it affects the *economy*, not just individuals.

So for example if I had to write two arguments about banning smoking, I would use a "big picture argument" for either side. Let's look at how I would THINK about it.

Note: This is just how I'd be thinking, <u>not how I'd actually write it:</u>

NO we should not ban smoking.

Money:

Right now the United States has many economic problems and two of the biggest problems are unemployment and underemployment. (Under employment means you are qualified for a better job but you can't find one so you work for less money. Example: a certified teacher who can only find a job as a substitute or paraprofessional.) *What would happen to all the people who work in the factories making the cigarettes if we suddenly banned cigarettes? What about the truckers that transport the product? What about the factory workers that make the packaging? What about the distributors? They would lose their jobs. And if they go on unemployment, who pays for it? Tax payers will have to pay for it. Not only do we have to consider the manufacturing workers, what about the farmers that grow the tobacco? How will it economically effect the farming industry? If you google "Economics of the Tobacco Industry" you will read some interesting information.*

Right now it's not sensible to ban smoking. It has far reaching implications in manufacturing and farming jobs. We can't afford the economic consequences.

Not only would it cause a problem in employment, cigarettes sales generate a lot of taxes for states and cities. For example the cost of a pack of cigarettes in Maryland is around $6 whereas the cost of a pack of cigarettes in NYC is around $12. This is because we tax the cigarettes at a higher rate in NYC and we use that tax money for public services. How much does the U.S. federal government make off taxes on cigarettes? $15,753,355,199 a year. That's over $15 billion dollars a year.

How does tobacco tax affect you? The President recently made plans to use the tax excise on cigarettes to provide $78 million dollars in Early Childhood Education funding. These taxes are being used for education as well.

YES we should ban smoking.

Money:

Smoking related illnesses, while treatable, are extremely expensive. Right now our country is facing the largest number of senior citizens that it's ever had. This generation is known as the "baby boom generation" because they were born right after World War II. By 2020 over 20% of our country will be senior citizens. Once a citizen turns 65 years old they are eligible for Medicare. What is Medicare?

Medicare is a program that provides health insurance for senior citizens in the United States when they retire. It doesn't matter how much money that senior citizen has, tax payers will be paying for their medical coverage.

Now imagine how expensive this is going to be for future generations. Senior citizens live longer these days and if they have a smoking related illness like cancer, heart disease or emphysema, the treatments can go on for decades. Can we afford this? Banning smoking now will save us billions of dollars in future medical treatments.

When I go over this with test takers the most common response is *"I would never have thought of that....how did you think of that? I can't think that way!"* But the interesting thing is that once you *do* start thinking this way you realize that these arguments show up all the time. You start to see in essays the ability to make arguments like this and suddenly it gets easier.

Stop and think about these "big picture arguments" for a second and consider two things. First, doesn't the argument that the packs of cigarettes are expensive for an individual person seem small in comparison? We're talking about people saving a couple of thousand dollars a year, versus millions or even billions of dollars a year. Second can you see a common point in both arguments?

TAX PAYERS

Most people have a tendency to overlook how much things actually cost tax payers in the country. When we change policies or run programs *the money has to come from somewhere.* It usually comes from taxes and that means WE are paying for it. Think about the recent decision to outfit all police officers with body cameras. On the one hand it's a great idea because it will impact the way police officers do their job. On the other hand it costs money to pay for it. It costs a lot of money and who is paying for it? <u>Tax payers.</u> Is it worth the cost?

A few years ago there was a decision to change all the street signs in NYC. What was the big change? The Federal Government ordered the signs to be changed to all UPPER CASE. So they changed all the signs to read like this: Houston St. to HOUSTON ST. Guess how much it cost to do this? $27.5 million. Guess who paid for it? **We did** as tax payers. So the question you want to ask yourself is if *it was worth the cost?*

I think most of us would consider the cameras on police officers as something that is worth the cost. It is a way of protecting citizens. It helps the police officer avoid bogus accusations of police brutality and protects them from unnecessary investigations at work. *(Which we also pay for.)* It saves us tax payers money in the long run because we avoid lengthy and expensive lawsuits. And it is a good gesture in showing that we care about the complaints about police misconduct in at-risk neighborhoods. That is worth the cost. Fancier street signs, not so much. Changing the street signs was a waste of tax payers' money.

Money Arguments to consider:

Taxes and tax payers: Who is paying for it? Will this policy save tax payers money or will it cost tax payers money in the long run? If it does, is it worth the cost? Is it a good investment of our money?

What are some of the things we pay for as tax payers?

- Education
- Welfare, Unemployment
- Maintaining roads and parks
- Law Enforcement
- Science research

Education:

Let's take a simple topic to consider the "bigger picture argument" related to a tax exemption for teachers: The Educator Expense Deduction. According to the IRS working educators are allowed to receive a tax deduction of $250 a year for classroom supplies, pencils, copies, books, computers, technologies. I can see you shaking your head right now thinking, *"$250 a year? That's a joke, I probably spend more money than that in two months!"* So let's consider an essay that asks:

"Should we raise the Educator Expense Deduction for teachers to $1,000 a year?"

If teachers are allowed to deduct this, it means that we as tax payers absorb that cost. We are saying, *"It's ok, you don't have to pay, we can afford to take the loss in tax revenue because we think it's worth it."* So what are some of the considerations about this topic?

As a society it benefits us in the long run to have properly equipped classrooms. We try to cover that cost in our school funding, but there are always times that a teacher, as an individual, will be able to see a specific need in their classroom. The big picture argument here is that it is **worth the cost** to make sure our children have all the supplies they need for school. Sometimes a "small issue" can have "big picture" consequences.

For example, think about how many parents/caregivers can't afford all the school supplies needed for school. Imagine a family that has several children. They go buy discount pencils from the 99 cents store, and then what happens when the student gets into the classroom? You as teachers know this well. Crappy pencils don't erase properly. They don't even write properly. Cheap notebooks will tear if the pages are crudely made. So instead of being able to focus on the lesson, the student is struggling just to take notes. Why? Because their parents couldn't afford proper school supplies.

A good pencil with a good eraser might cost a little bit more, but it has a far reaching impact in the classroom. Isn't it worth it for teachers to be able to stock up on good pencils and then deduct it from their taxes at the end of the year? A pencil is a tiny economic expense that can effect a student's education in a big way. School supplies are important and have a "big picture impact" on Education costs.

Remember when we discussed **ROI** or Return on Investment in the section on charts? Today's students are our future. They are worth the investment. It is completely worth the cost to allow teachers to deduct more in their Educator Expenses so that they can properly supply their classrooms.

One way to do some research on what these kinds of arguments sound like is to watch Youtube video clips from television shows like 20/20 and 60 minutes. These clips are generally just a few minutes long and they quickly go over these kinds of arguments in the episode. My favorite person to watch is named John Stossel. He has many Youtube clips that relate to topics that are usually chosen for any standardized exam that is used in high schools. When I taught SAT prep I used these all the time. You should look for "Stossel in The Classroom" or just type in his name and the topic you want to investigate.

There are a few favorites I'd recommend:

- "Needy Seniors or Greedy Geezers"
- "Global Warming Debate"

I don't necessarily agree with all his arguments but you can't deny that he has a great style of debating.

Extending the Argument

Many of my students have lost points because they didn't realize they had to "extend the argument beyond the passages." This is a requirement on the NYSTCE ALST Rubric. Go look it up online. Extending the argument proves to the evaluator that you really understand what the TOPIC is about, not just what is written in the Passages. Now remember that you are only writing about 5 sentences in paragraphs 2 and 3 when discussing your reasons.

- Sentence 1: State your position.
- Sentence 2: Explain your reasoning.
- Sentence 3: Cite from the article
- Sentence 4: Explain how this backs up your claim.
- Sentence 5: Sum up your point.

Are you starting to realize how simple these essays are supposed to be? It's ok to add more sentences but it is never ok to use less. So where would you "extend your argument" within those five sentences? Well you can't do it in sentence 1, 3, or 5 can you? **So you do it in sentence 2 or sentence 4.** Remember it's OK if you use an extra sentence to extend the argument. But you must show them that you have considered and understand the topic beyond what is written in the Passages.

For example, let's consider an argument about whether or not we should use robots or doctors to perform surgery. We'll use two short "Passages."

Passage A*: Linda Cartell "Doctors Must Be the Surgeons"*

The advances in medicine over the last few decades has shown us the importance of allowing Doctors to take risks, perform surgeries and work with patients. Doctors have trained for years and are able to quickly respond to the nuances in surgery in ways that robots would not be able to do.

Every surgery a doctor performs is not only a moment where they heal a patient, it is the opportunity for that doctor and his staff to learn more in ways that are beyond the capabilities of a robot. There are innovations in medicine based on new diagnoses, new understanding and new techniques. These things can only be done at the hand of a well-trained doctor. Indeed training for a doctor is a life-long endeavor.

Passage B: *David Shekore "Robots are Life Savers in More Ways than One."*

The practical implications of robotic surgery cannot be ignored. Not only is a robot more precise in its technique, it does not suffer from many of the issues that would affect a doctor. Robots don't get tired, they don't have shaky hands and they don't sweat which can impair vision. In short, robots are less likely to make mistakes and more like to perform well under pressure.

Not only do robots make sense from a performance position, they also make more sense from an economic one. Robots are safer to use. Not only do hospitals avoid costly malpractice suits for complications that arise in surgery, they eliminate the possibility of doctors contracting illnesses while performing surgery. The slip of a scalpel on a patient with a blood transferable disease can not only endanger a doctor's life but essentially end their career. As technology continues to improve in the world we should take advantage of smarter, cheaper and safer ways to help patients.

Let's look at a student's essay and how she "extended the argument." The bolded sections below show that the writer understood the topic in general and uses examples NOT mentioned in the Passages.

Sample excerpt from an essay:

Advances in technology have paved the way for robotic replacements of many professionals, including even doctors and surgeons. Critics opposed to the use of robotics in the medical field contend that there is no substitute for human doctors who can diagnose illness with the benefit of experience, and relate to how their patients feel. Proponents point out that robots are not likely to make errors, are more immune to risk factors and are an economically sound choice. The use of robots in the field of medicine is worthy of consideration. There are times when robots are a valid alternative to medical professionals that makes medical treatment safer and more affordable.

First, the use of robots can prevent doctors, surgeons and nurses from being placed at unnecessary risk. In the article "Robots are Life Savers in More Ways than One," David Shekore points out that "the slip of a scalpel on a patient with a blood transferable disease can not only endanger a doctor's life, but essentially end their career." **Robots would make working with patients who have Ebola less risky, and eliminate the need for self-contained suits**

that impair care. These examples show that robotics are a practical solution that improves the safety of our medical staff, and the future patients they come in contact with. For this reason alone, it is well worth the relatively minor inconvenience of losing some face-to-face interaction with doctors, to make medical treatment safer for all.

Second, robots in the medical field could help reduce the high cost of medical care. Malpractice suits for complications that result from medical mistakes, such as David Shekore points out, are not the only cost factors robotics could reduce. **By placing doctors, surgeons, nurses and ultimately patients at less risk of contamination, common infections associated with long hospital stays such as MRSA could potentially be reduced. Infections account for more days in the hospital for patients recovering from surgery, and more time in the hospital means greater costs.** Robots are not at risk of infection, nor of making errors. Therefore, they are an economic benefit to both those practicing medicine and those being treated.

Can you see in the above bolded how the writer explains their position by using examples that they may have read about in newspapers or have seen in the news? This shows the evaluator that you have a real understanding of the topic and are not just parroting back what the writers of the Passages are saying. You must extend the arguments in Essay 3.

You should try to think of ways that the topics relate to information that you have heard about outside the parameters of the information given in the test. Be careful to avoid dramatic or anecdotal examples, they are not very strong arguments.

Paragraph 4: The Counter Claim

I encourage writers to use Paragraph 4 to make their counter claim. It's a good place for it, and if you consider Paragraph 4 your "counter claim paragraph," then you won't forget to do it. It's also a great place to cite the chart. On this Essay you are supposed to cite all three sources: Passage A, Passage B and the chart. Since paragraphs 2 and 3 are going to use one of the passages that backs up your claims, the best place to cite the other passage and the chart is in the fourth paragraph. It also helps break up your argument so that you don't sound repetitive in the conclusion.

What is a counter claim? Many of my students misunderstand what a counter claim means. They think it means something like this:

On the other hand, I can also see what John Smith is saying in the other Passage. He makes a good point that we should consider other variables when evaluating the effectiveness of child car seat use in cars. He says that the risks are exaggerated and that older children who are frustrated by being so tightly restrained in a car seat will often become more of a distraction to the driver than if they are allowed to sit on the seat with a seatbelt. This is an interesting observation and the writer backs up his argument with citations from the National Association of Children in Cars.

Nope! That is not what a counter claim means. A counter claim means that you consider what the other side or "claim" is and you "counter it" or "prove it wrong." You have to first show that you clearly understand the point the writer is making, but then you debate it and prove it wrong.

I'll write two counter claims on the topic of "banning smoking."

Pro Ban Smoking

Reason 1 Health Consequences

Reason 2 Economic costs of Medicare related to smoking.

Counter claim:

In John Doe's article entitled, "We Cannot Afford to Ban Smoking" he points out that smoking related risks are greatly exaggerated in the U.S. and that, in reality, more people are at risk of dying from diabetes related illnesses than smoking. Doe uses the example of Mayor Bloomberg's attempt to ban soft drinks as an example of the government overstepping its bounds and trying to interfere with people's personal decisions. While this is a good point, he seems to equivocate "drinking soft drinks" with "smoking." They are not the same thing; what you drink only effects your own body. Smoking in public also affects other people and can cause illnesses in people who never smoked a day in their life. As we can see in the chart entitled "Respiratory Illnesses in Smokers" there is an increase in respiratory illnesses in children in homes where the parents are smokers. This underscores the how smoking is no longer just a personal issue but a public responsibility.

Con Ban Smoking

Reason 1 Economic consequences

Reason 2 Infringement of personal choices

Counter claim:

In Alison David's essay entitled "Where There's Smoke There's Problems" she points out that it is important to ban smoking because it will greatly reduce crime in our country. She explains that deviant behavior like smoking encourages young people to take risks and creates more crime. While this is an understandable concern, the history of our country has shown that any time the government has attempted to control what people do by outright banning things, crime has skyrocketed as a result. We only need to consider the consequences of Prohibition in the United States or our current War on Drugs to see the results. These attempted solutions have only created more crime and have never lowered the number of people using the banned substance. As we can see in the chart entitled "Respiratory Illnesses in Smokers," the vast majority of people smoking are not young criminal teenagers, but adults who have chosen to take the risk.

The purpose of a counter claim is to show the reader that you are not "ranting" about a topic but are carefully and logically evaluating both sides. This type of debating is part of the common core standard. If a teacher doesn't know how to do it, then how can they teach a student to do it?

The counter claim has three parts

- What would the other side say that disagrees with me? Explain it.
- Prove it wrong and make a claim.
- Back up that claim using evidence in the chart.

The Conclusion

The conclusion is generally the easiest part of the essay to write. I also think they cut you a little slack because they assume you are running out of time. But if you use the Five Sentence model you will be able to quickly jot it down. In this paragraph you go by ideas rather than specific sentences.

- Summarize the main points made in your essay in 2 sentences.
- Repeat your thesis in a reworded format.
- Leave off with a cautionary or encouraging statement that points out that you are correct.

In conclusion, it is clear that using child car seats while driving, is a law that should be upheld. Child car seats save lives, prevent injuries and minimize the economic costs related to these issues. Like mandatory seat belt laws, this policy is easily enforced and will grow to be customary over time. Parents should be trained on how to properly install and use these effective devices. With the increased number of distracted drivers on the road, it is important to take every precaution to ensure the safety of children in cars.

The only two mistakes that writers generally make in the conclusion is that they start sounding too repetitive or they bring up a new idea. Try to keep it simple. This is not the part of the essay where you want to impress people. This paragraph is just about wrapping up all your ideas and ending the essay.

Sample Sets

CAUTION! When I published my last test prep book and it first came out almost all of my students received very high scores on the essays. The book was a huge success for the first two years after publication.

However, over time, no matter how many times I told people not to copy the essays, they kept doing it. The scores went from 260 and 300 to 180 and 140. This is failing. How could the same template suddenly cause people to fail? Eventually I realized that it seemed the evaluators started recognizing the strategies and treating the essays as a template. I don't know how the evaluators think, I can only go by the scores. It seemed to me that they felt that the essays were being copied, instead of being written originally.

So in order to prevent plagiarism, I'm only including unrelated essays here. I know if I don't put sample essays in the book, people will be confused, but they are just something to look at to get an idea. Do not copy the wording or you will fail.

Essay 1 (Word count 194)

In Billy Bonkers article entitled "Don't Copy the Essays" he explains that plagiarism is a very common problem in schools and that more needs to be done to prevent this from happening. He further contends that many students don't even realize they are plagiarizing and therefore more needs to be done to address this issue. Bonkers points out the long term consequences related to plagiarism and how it can impact a teacher's career.

In contrast Jolly Jiggles argues in his article, "Much Ado about Copying" that in this day and age copying information is not really plagiarizing. He points out that that because of the internet it is not really possible to claim originality of ideas. And he further contends that the nature of writing has changed because of the viral nature of internet conversations.

Although both authors make compelling points, Jiggles backs up his points with evidence from the National Association from the Arts. He uses logical deduction rather than emotions in making his points. Bonkers does make strong arguments but he only uses one citation and a quote to back up these claims. Therefore Jiggles makes a stronger argument for his position.

Essay 2 (Word count 218)

When examining the chart entitled "People Copy all the Time" we can see that there has been an increase in the number of test takers that copy wording out of books, templates and use ideas that are not their own. From 2007 until 2009 this number has increased by 30%. The comparative chart entitled "Number of Students Failing Tests" shows an increase of 40% in the same time period. We can conclude that there is a correlation between plagiarism and failing the test.

This evidence contradicts Jolly Jiggles article "Much Ado about Copying" in which he states that there are no real long term problems associated with plagiarism. Jiggles suggests that the world is changing, and while this may be true, at the current time students are failing at the same rate they are copying. This can affect a teacher's ability to pass a test and ultimately prevent them from becoming certified. When a teacher struggles to pass an exam that is a necessary requirement, it can have a long term impact on their ability to get a job in teaching. Additionally a teacher who repeatedly fails a tests is less likely to be considered to be a strong candidate when applying for a job. Jolly Jiggles is minimizing a very significant problem in the field of education.

Essay 3 (Word count 609)

Writing is considered a creative expression of original thoughts and ideas. For many writers, avoiding plagiarism is a matter of choosing integrity over convenience. However, in the modern world of Google and Wikipedia, research on unfamiliar topics often yields a tempting amount of anonymous information. Yet, no one wants to be accused of assuming credit for someone else's work. Therefore, harsh punishments are needed to ensure academic integrity and to develop critical thinking skills in writers.

Firstly, academic integrity is a fundamental construct of learning. In Billy Bonker's article "Don't Copy the Essays" he points out how common a problem plagiarism is in schools. Although copying another student's work word-for-word is universally considered cheating, using other's ideas is not always associated with plagiarism. The use of templates and examples of other's writing can contribute to students growing accustomed to using other people's ideas as their own. Students are then often taken by surprise when severe penalties are levied for plagiarism. Failing a test for certification is one of the most severe penalties, with consequences of not only looking bad, but being denied future employment in one's chosen field.

In addition, stealing credit for other people's ideas also robs the student who copies of the chance to develop their own critical thinking skills. Billy Bonkers states in his article that "this is perhaps the worst penalty of all. We know longer learn how to think for ourselves." Bonkers describes a professor who gave out a template to help his students organize their writing. However 22 out of 25 students simply copied the wording instead of using the template to help guide their writing. Professor Hardnose stated that each of these students "failed to answer the most important question" because they simply copied his template, and "missed the point of the entire exercise!" This is an example of how copying what others have written denies the student the opportunity to even form an original thought of their own, or gain an understanding of the material.

Conversely, many students don't consider copying information as being a form of cheating. Jolly Jiggles states in his article "Much Ado about Copying" that the "viral nature of internet conversations" has changed the "nature of writing." He contends that the internet makes it impossible to "claim originality of ideas." Despite Mr. Jiggles' claims that copying information is a normal part of academic success and has no side effects, statistics show that those who plagiarize tend to fail more often than those who don't. In the chart "People Copy all the Time" rates of students failing tests increases by 40%, as rates of students who copy wording and ideas has risen by 30%. It's possible that the students who don't copy are under more pressure to truly understand the material they are learning, while students who simply copy never need to form their own thoughts and ideas.

In conclusion, plagiarism is detrimental to students, regardless of whether or not they are ever caught. The requirements in academic writing, such as citing other writer's as a source, exposes students to any number of negative consequences when they fail to give credit properly. Copying information about a topic can also prevent a student from ever thinking about the material long enough to understand it themselves. Although there is an overabundance of anonymous information available on the internet, and not citing it properly may never be discovered, statistics show that casual plagiarism still makes students more likely to fail. Finally, it is not simply a matter of right and wrong, but also a matter of gaining necessary critical thinking ability that makes plagiarism something to be avoided in one's writing.

	Rubric for Essay 3	1	2	3	4
1	Essays are within the word count range				
2	There are five paragraphs				
3	Introduction is at least five sentences				
4	Introduction has a topic sentence that explains the issue being discussed.				
5	Introduction has a thesis statement that takes a side and states two reasons to be discussed				
6	Paragraphs have at least five sentences				
7	Paragraphs 2, 3, 4, 5 use transitional phrases				
8	Paragraphs 2, 3, 4 cite the passages given on the test				
9	Paragraphs 2, 3, 4 extend the argument by giving examples that are not in the passages				
10	Paragraph 4 addresses the counterclaim				
11	Paragraph 4 cites the chart				
12	Conclusion repeats arguments made in paragraphs 2, 3, 4				
13	Grammar is correct				
14	Voice is clear and professional. The writer sounds like they understand and care about the topic				
15	Sophisticated vocabulary and sentence structure is used				
	Total				
	Divided by 15				

PART 2: HOW TO FAIL YOUR ESSAYS!

Alligator Blood!

AKA Plagiarism

One of the worst mistakes that some people make after taking my class is that they plagiarize without realizing they are doing it. I can tell when they have done this on the test because they come back with *1 plus* on the essay. Stop and think about how a person could sit in a prep class, practice writing, get evaluations and then go down and get *1 plus* on the essay? Many times they had previously received two pluses prior to the class. So obviously something went very wrong. I use the example of *"alligator blood"* to explain this concept and I want you to remember it! This is why you *must* practice writing your essay off the top of your head over and over again before you take the test.

Most people understand that if you copy someone's *words* and try to pass them off as your own, this is considered plagiarism. But many people don't realize that if you copy someone else's *ideas* and try to pass them off on your own it is also **plagiarism.**

The topic we were discussing in class was whether or not Florida should put a stop to home construction that encroaches into wildlife habitats. In the class we went over several ideas about the economic impact and "big picture ideas" related to this topic. At one point we began discussing the importance of preserving the natural habitats of animals because they are part of ecosystems that can impact human life. Then I asked the students to take out their phones and google these words:

Alligator blood HIV

My students were surprised to find out that recent research in the field of medicine had discovered that the antibodies in Alligator Blood were being used to create a cure for HIV. Wow! Imagine that! Take a second to google "Alligator blood HIV" to read some information.

After this discussion students went home to practice writing their essays and over the next few days I received essays that included the three examples below:

Example 1

The importance of preserving the natural habitats of animals in Florida is very important. In fact recent studies have shown that alligator blood is now being used to find a cure for cancer. If we don't protect alligators we are throwing away life-saving possibilities.

Example 2

Although John Smith argues that the housing needs of people in these areas outweigh the needs of animals he is overlooking something very important. Many of these animals have unknown uses in science that could one day save lives. For example new research in the field of HIV has recently discovered that antibodies in alligator blood may one day be the cure for HIV. We must protect these animals because we never know what the future may bring.

Example 3

Precious resources are often discovered in protected natural habitats. For example bats in certain areas eat mosquitoes which help prevent the spread of disease. In addition medical research has now found that the cure for HIV may be as close as alligator blood. Studies have concluded that antibodies in alligator blood hold a clue to discovering the cure. Imagine if we had not discovered this before we destroyed their environment?

This is **plagiarism.** None of these students thought of this idea on their own. They took my idea and tried to pass it off as their own. And it is very possible that there is an algorithm programmed into the computer system that "red flags" an essay for plagiarism. You will notice that throughout this book, any time I have used someone else's idea I have <u>always</u> cited the source of the idea. I didn't just reword it and pretend it was my own idea.

Imagine if these three students had gone in and taken the test around the same time? How noticeable would it be? Was it noticeable to you? They all got 1 plus on their essay. It's a shame too, because in Essay 3 the writer made a good original point about the bats. If they had stuck with their own idea instead of stealing mine, they would have done quite well.

Another problem that test takers have is that because they don't practice writing their essay; when they get down there and try to think of ideas and arguments they freeze up and can only remember what I said in the classroom. So they write what *I said,* instead of their own ideas. It is blatant and it's tantamount to cheating. This is why I also encourage people not to prep for a test with a friend.

I had once had two women who went to take the test together. They had sat up all night talking about ideas. One of the ideas actually related to the essay they both got. Do you think the friend who didn't think of the idea was responsible enough to say *"Well that was really Jenny's idea, I'm sure she'll use it so I'll think of something else."* Of course not. Mary took Jenny's idea and used it in her essay. Mary finished first and left. When the scores came out Mary got 3 pluses on her essay and Jenny got 1 plus on hers. The weird thing was that Jenny was definitely the better writer so I can only assume that the test evaluator thought Jenny copied off Mary.

Not only can you fail the test if you do this, you can get yourself banned from taking the test again which means in essence you can never become a certified teacher in NY.

The ideas in this book are designed to help you start thinking about your OWN ideas, they are not here for you to use and try to pass off as your own. If you do and you get 1 plus on your essay, don't come complaining to me. You have been warned. Just remember: **Alligator Blood!**

Not Baking the Cookies!

AKA Not Writing the Essay

People always want to call me on the phone and talk about the essay. You can sound brilliant on the phone but if you don't write the essay, I have no idea how you will do on the test. You should practice each set of essays, (but especially Essay 3) three times. Write it—write it-- write it-- write it--write it. Don't talk about it, ***write it.***

Think of this test like a BAKE OFF for Cookies

- *Tyron Johnson has a fantastic cookie recipe that has been passed down in his family for generations. He memorizes the cookie recipe and bakes a batch one time and they come out burnt so he thinks, "ok I know what I did wrong, when I get down there I'll be more careful. I got it, next time I'll watch them more closely." He bakes another batch of cookies and they come out great!*
- *Jennifer Smith has a good cookie recipe and she bakes a batch of cookies. It doesn't come out so tasty. So she changes the recipe a little and bakes another batch. Still not quite good. She bakes 6 more batches of cookies. She's practicing baking cookies over and over again. Finally she thinks she's got a good recipe and so she bakes two more batches for practice.*

When Tyron and Jennifer get down to the bake off they have to bake the cookies again ***right there from scratch*** and they cannot look at the recipe. Who do you think is going to win?

This is the biggest problem I can't quite get you writers to understand. You have to be able to bake the cookies **when you get there.** It's **not** about bringing in a "winning recipe" plate of cookies to the Bake Off. It's about _baking them_ at the site. You could have made amazing cookies at home. But those cookies are useless at a bake off because you have to bake a new batch of cookies again. They don't care about the great cookies at home. They don't care about your great-grandmother's prize winning recipe. They only care about the cookies you are **baking right now.**

Now imagine that they ask the contestants to bake a different kind of cookie. Who do you think is going to win?

Jennifer is more likely to win because she's practiced doing it over and over again. Even though Tyron might have a great recipe at home, he doesn't have it there with him. He could have boxes of amazing cookies at home. Just like you have folders of great essays and straight "A"s on all your college essays. But because Tyron did not practice he will probably lose. Just like you will likely fail if you don't practice writing the essays. You have been warned!

Practice baking your cookies over and over again!

Comma Queens!!!

A comma queen is a writer who writes really long drawn out sentences with lots and lots of commas. The sentences are run on sentences and don't make any sense. I always tell my students: ONE IDEA ONE SENTENCE. ELL writers are especially notorious for this. Here's an example:

President Weiman's farewell address is one of the most important, historical, American speeches regardless explaining the forward strategies to face the series of warning, motivating, understanding, and instructing the people.

What? Try reading that three times.

One idea One Sentence

President Weiman's Farewell Address is one of the most important speeches in history. It is a warning to the people. The President's speech motivated people during the Cold War.

Even though this is weak, at least you understand what the person is trying to say. ONE IDEA ONE SENTENCE. And notice how she kept trying to use "fancy words" instead of just explaining it simply. Don't do this!

Thesaurus Trolls!!!

Remember Viktor? Viktor failed because his writing was so convoluted that readers couldn't understand his points. Another problem writers make is trying to "fancy up" their writing by going to the thesaurus and picking a word that they think means the same thing to make the writing sound smarter.

Stop right now and do something. Go to Youtube on either your phone or computer. Once you are on Youtube type in this search "Joey Friends Adoption Letter" The clip should be a little over 2 minutes long. It's a funny clip because he tried to rewrite an entire letter with a thesaurus so he'd "sound smarter." He doesn't sound smarter; he sounds like an idiot.

I've also watched students in class try to use a translator to translate the wording from their home language to English. Why you are doing this makes absolutely no sense to me. First of all the translation is never correct and there are nuances in languages that don't translate properly. When people do this we get essays with sentences like this:

The use of the car seat for progenies attended driving should be banned because is unsafe and provoke an increment in the community expenditure.

What? Seriously, what? Just use plain English. You will definitely lose a few points for not using sophisticated sentences and words, but you will fail the entire essay if you write something like this. When I spoke to the girl in the class and asked her what she meant she said, *"I meant parents should always use a car seat for their children because it's much safer and medical treatments are expensive."*

I think maybe that day you heard me beating my head against the wall. Why didn't she just say that? That would have been fine!

Do not be a Thesaurus Troll!

Drama Queens!!!

For some reason, bad writers seem to think that they can make a stronger argument if they write things that sound very dramatic. You don't make a stronger argument. You sound ridiculously out of touch with reality. Remember when we discussed the economic impact of banning smoking? I had two different Drama Queens write arguments based on that topic:

Example 1

The long term impact of banning cigarettes would mean a devastation of the tobacco farmer. Farms that had been in families for generations would completely collapse and they would be abandoned desolate wastelands in once strong communities. By the end of the decade the entire area will look like Detroit with poverty, crime and homelessness everywhere. The cigarette ban has the power to destroy this country.

Um....really?

Example 2

The United States is facing a huge job shortage. More and more jobs are being lost in the medical field. It is important that we try to help doctors and nurses keep their jobs. The more people who smoke, the more there will be a need for these important jobs. Banning smoking will ultimately result in the thousands of professionals being out on the street with no job and no future.

Ok now first of all this is a total Drama Queen argument. Doctors and nurses will probably be able to find other jobs. It's not going to be *that* bad! But basically her argument seems to be that we should hope people get cancer so doctors and nurses keep their jobs? Really?

And one of my favorites about whether or not Physical Education should be taught in schools:

Example 3

Physical activities in the schools help them during disaster management like in a flood situation. If students learn to swim, they can save their own lives and rescue others. We saw many lost lives in Hurricane Sandy that could have been avoided if children were able to do rescue. We should not underestimate how important this life saving skill is in life.

So in other words, we should teach physical education so that kids can be mobilized as a rescue force during a disaster like a flood or hurricane. Really? We'll just toss the kids out into a hurricane with their little life vests on and tell them to start rescuing people! Right? Oh my.

Don't do this. For the love of all that is sane, don't do this!!

Working with a partner and taking the test around the same time!

Guess what happens when you and a partner work together? One of you fails the other one passes. This is because the "nicer" friend spends time trying to help the other friend.

And guess who always fails? The nice friend! I have watched this happen over and over and over again. There are two reasons this can happen. One is that you take the test too close together and the evaluator recognizes the essays as similar and fails one person for copying off the other.

The other reason is because as nice and brilliant as you think you are, you are helping the other person deal with their issues instead of focusing on your own. On tests BE SELFISH. Take care of yourself first. Do not share your work with ANYONE until you have passed the test.

Tips to Help You Stay Organized

Follow the format not a template.

Too often students sit in my class and create a "template" and then try to use the "template" to write the essay. When they do this they always fail. You can't just memorize certain phrases and sentences and jam them into the essay wherever. It reads exactly like that. You don't sound like you are writing the essay. You sound like you memorized something and are trying to copy it and are not really writing.

The essay must be a cohesive, organized, fluid piece of writing that is focused, cites the sources, gives extra examples to expand the argument and follows the structure of an argumentative essay. For example, when I get an essay and it has 2 sentences in the introduction, I don't even bother reading the rest of it. FAIL! If you have never evaluated essays, you don't know what it's like to read them. Evaluators give the essay a 30 second glance at first and if it doesn't follow the format they will fail it from the start.

Follow the format.

Narrow down what you need to be doing by paragraph.

- Paragraph 1 Introduce the topic, thesis statement
- Paragraph 2 Discuss ONE point and cite the sources, give an extra example to expand the argument
- Paragraph 3 Discuss a different point and cite the sources, give an extra example to expand the argument

- Paragraph 4 Counterclaim Explain the counter claim, cite the sources and the chart, prove it wrong, give an extra example to expand the argument
- Paragraph 5 summarize your points in five separate sentences. Reword the thesis at the end.

Know your weaknesses.

I am a horrible speller. You may have noticed in the classroom that I will always ask people to check if I spelled a word correctly. Because of this I know I need to go back and edit my writing and double check. There is not a spell check on these tests so I know that I need to be super careful. When I take tests like this I will always write the essay first, then do the multiple choice and then go back and look at my writing to check for mistakes. You should do the same thing. You need to take a break in your writing so that you can re-read your essay from a fresh perspective.

Doing the multiple choice will give you a break from your essay and allow you to read something else and then go back. Do the test in this order:

A. Write the essays first
B. Then go do the multiple choice
C. Then go back and edit your essay.

Memorize the rubric not the essay.

If you memorize the rubric you will be able to edit yourself wisely. As you continue to practice writing you should constantly use the rubric to evaluate your writing. This way on the day of the test you will be able to do the same thing. Please keep in mind that the ideas I have suggested in these workshops are simplified versions of what you should be doing on the test. You should not adhere to them if you are a strong writer, but instead use them as a guideline. The single most important thing they are looking for on this essay is an organized professional piece of writing. The rubric will help you stay focused and hit all the points.

VOICE

This is something that is very difficult to teach. Most poor writers sound like they are just listing a series of sentences with no real understanding or interest in the topic. Even though you won't fail with a weak "voice" in your writing, you can earn points if you sound like you actually care about the topic in your writing. Think about why you like this book. (I sure hope you do!) Most people tell me that the "voice" in the book is conversational and accessible. But I explain things as clearly as possible.

Be consistent.

If you start off sounding professional and academic, stay with that voice. If you start off sounding professional and relatable, stay with that voice. The voice should always sound professional.

And one more word of caution. Do not discuss race, gender or religious beliefs in your essay. It will <u>always go wrong.</u> A recent example of this mistake would be this one written about the topic regarding the Educator Expenditure Deduction:

As we know poor blacks can't always afford to buy good pencils for their kids and this is a problem in school that causes issues with learning.

OUCH! I know that in this book I used some examples that involved racism. I did so to make a dramatic point in a test prep guide. I would never ever on a test write anything like that because you never know who is reading your essay and it could be taken the wrong way. This writer's example reads extremely racist to me and I'd be annoyed while reading the rest of the essay. Consider that you are trying to get certified as a teacher. They don't want racists, sexists or religious fanatics in the classroom. You won't pass.

Also note that this is an example of Alligator Blood. The writer totally stole my idea of the pencil and tried to pass it off as their own. Nope!

Explain your extended arguments.

Don't just "insert them" in the essay. When you are trying to extend an argument by showing you understand the topic, you should be sure to clearly explain your example and how it relates to the points made in the passages. You also want to choose examples that back up your claims.

Use Transitions:

Transitions are words and phrases that connect ideas and show how they are related. There are a list of common transitions on the next two pages. To repeat an idea just stated:

- In other words,
- That is,
- To repeat,
- Again,

To illustrate an idea:

- For example,
- For instance,
- In particular,
- To illustrate,
- In this manner,
- Thus

To announce a contrast, a change in direction:

- Yet,
- However,
- Still,
- Nevertheless,
- On the other hand,
- In contrast,
- Instead of,
- On the contrary,
- Conversely,
- Notwithstanding,
- In spite of this,

Time:

- At once,
- In the interim,
- At length,
- Immediately,
- To sum up,
- At last,
- Meanwhile,
- In the meantime,
- Presently,
- At the same time,
- Shortly,
- In the end,
- Temporarily,
- Thereafter,

To restate an idea more precisely:

- To be exact,
- To be specific,
- To be precise,
- More specifically,
- More precisely,

To mark a new idea as an addition to what has been said:

- Similarly,
- Also,
- Too,

- Besides,
- Furthermore,
- Further,
- Moreover,
- In addition,
- To show cause and effect:
- As a result,
- For this reason,
- Therefore,
- Hence,
- Consequently,
- Accordingly,

Conclusion:

- In short,
- To conclude,
- In brief,
- On the whole,

Generalities of Writing Mistakes by American and ESOL Writers:

These writing mistakes are related to how you come up with ideas, how you explain the ideas and your logic and reasoning in your essays. We will also touch on typical grammar errors.

Americans

American writers have the highest fail rate with me because they don't practice writing the essay. They constantly want to talk to me about writing it but they don't write it. It's actually really annoying. I guess the mindset is, *"I know how to write and now that I understand it I'm good to go. How hard can it be?"* It's hard people. It's **really** hard. You have to practice before you go down. And practice doesn't mean, write one essay and have it edited and then fix it. You have to write it off the top of your head over and over again, not rewrite an edited essay. This is not a term paper. You shouldn't even be looking at your original draft when you write the next one. You won't be able to do that at the test site will you? So you can't practice that way.

The other mistake that American writers make is confusing the term *citizens* with tax payers. You don't have to be a citizen to be a tax payer. Many of the topics on these types of tests are ones that are about social policies. Not all people who live in the US are citizens. In fact, some of them have no intention of ever becoming one.

I personally know people who lived here for 10 years or so who are not citizens. Don't you? They are **residents,** *customers, consumers, people, members of society, home owners, educators, tax payers, etc.* but they are not citizens. Don't use citizens in your essays unless you specifically mean citizens. For example if you were discussing voting, then you mean citizens because only citizens can vote. But if you are talking about changing school policies, that doesn't just apply to citizens.

That Which Who

American writers tend to confuse when you should use these terms. I guess it is because in casual conversation it's never corrected. Sometimes evaluators don't even notice this type of mistake but if you get someone who does, you can lose points.

I tell my teachers to remember these phrases and to use them as a mnemonic device:

That witches broom

That and which are about objects or animals.

Who is people

For example if you read this sentence you probably wouldn't notice the mistake:

- ***I gave the papers to the security guard that was sitting at the desk.***

This is wrong. It should be:

- *I gave the papers to the security guard **who** was sitting at the desk.*
- *I placed the papers in the box **that** was sitting on the desk.*
- *I gave the bone to the dog **that** was sitting by the couch.*

In the essays I often see mistakes like this:

- *When considering the economic impact that this policy will have on tax payers **that** own cars, it is important to look at the big picture.*

This is wrong. It should be:

- *When considering the economic impact that this policy will have on tax payers **who** own cars, it is important to look at the big picture.*

Using "which" is done with specific rules so I'd just avoid it altogether. Remember I'm not trying to get you to be an amazing writer, just to pass the test.

Contractions:

I generally advise students never to use contractions. Most of us don't even realize when we use them wrong in typing because autocorrect catches them and automatically fixes them when we are writing. There is no autocorrect on the test. So try to always spell out both words. This problem has been made worse by shortcuts used in texting. Be careful.

- *Its (possessive)*
- *It's (It is)*
- *Your*
- *You're (you are)*
- *Their*
- *They're (they are)*
- *There (place)*

John and I versus John and me.

You know that annoying facebook friend that corrects your grammar all the time? Yep that's me. I can't help myself. I try, really I do. But it drives me up the wall when I see people making this mistake when posting facebook pictures.

Here's an easy way to keep it straight.

If you can replace it with WE it's *John and I.*

- John and I are going camping!
- **We** are going camping.

If you can replace it with US it's *John and me.*

- David Hoff just gave John and I free passes to his concert!

Nope!

- David Hoff just gave **we** free passes to his concert!

That doesn't make any sense does it?

- David Hoff just gave **us** free passes to his concert!
- David Hoff just gave John and me free passes to his concert!

Misunderstanding when to use a semicolon.

For some reason a lot of people think a semicolon is an "alternative" to a colon. It's not. It's an alternative to a comma or period. I always tell students to remember what it looks like.

; (see it's got a comma and period!)

Let's look at the sentence below

Mary's party was great, it lasted until the morning.

Many people wouldn't catch this mistake. It's called a "comma splice." A comma splice is a mistake when you are connecting two whole sentences with a comma instead of a semicolon. Basically the only time you really use a semicolon is when you are listing things or when you are connecting two complete sentences.

Mary's party was great.

This is a complete sentence.

It lasted until the morning.

This is a complete sentence.

You could use a period and make it two separate sentences. But when you connect two complete sentences you use a semicolon, not a comma.

Mary's party was great; it lasted until the morning.

There are other rules for this but this is the most common mistake I see. You can look up more online if you wish.

ESOL Writers

I have taught these tests for so many years that I've been able to notice patterns typical to certain cultures and languages. These are generalizations that have shown up in the essay evaluations. I thought I'd break it down by culture to help you get a more specific insight. This doesn't mean if you are from this culture you will definitely make this mistake. But I wanted to share these observations with you just in case.

Asian (Chinese, Japanese, Korean, Indian, Pakistani)

Asian writers have a tendency to be too "nice" in Essay 3. The writing is usually very diplomatic and well thought out, until we get to Paragraph 4 and the counter claim. In that paragraph the number one problem my writers have is in not understanding that they have to strongly disagree with the statements that the other side has made. If I see this phrase in an essay, *"on the other hand,"* it's usually written by an Asian writer. And they usually just ***explain*** the other side instead of disagreeing with it. You must ***debate*** and prove the claim wrong. These writers tend to forget to do this.

Asian writers also often tend to struggle with understanding when you use capitals, the word "the" and when you should use the letter "s" in a verb tense.

Example: government

- The government helps the people. (correct)
- Government helps the people. (wrong)
- The government helps people. (correct)
- Government help people. (wrong)

Example: governor

- The governor helps the people. (correct)
- The Governor help people. (wrong)
- The Governor helps people. (wrong)
- The governor helps people. (correct)
- Governor Johnson helps the people. (correct)

You should not capitalize the word *"government"* unless it is the first word of the sentence. You should not capitalize the word *"governor"* when it is used as a noun. Only when it is used as a title.

Example:

- President Obama gave a speech. (correct)
- Obama is the President. (wrong)
- Obama is the president. (correct)
- The President is coming to visit. (wrong)
- The president is coming to visit. (correct)
- President Obama is coming to visit. (correct)
- The President Obama is coming to visit. (wrong)

My advice to you is to pick one way that you are going to use the phrase and use it the same way each time. Don't change it around or you will likely get confused and make a mistake.

Eastern European (Russian, Ukrainian, Georgian)

Eastern European writers write long sentences more than my other groups of writers. I have been told by several of my Russian students that this is how they are taught to write in Russian.

For example if I see a sentence like this:

"The possibilities for the endless discoveries in the Alaskan wilderness as they are uncovered, investigated, explored, and examined, creates a meaningful history of scientific, environmental, ecological, biological, chemical and naturalistic research that can benefit future generations in the fields of Science, Health and Geological Development."

If I see a sentence like that, it will usually have been written by an Eastern European writer. It's not **wrong**, but it's too much. I think the biggest misconception that these writers have is that they think that some really intelligent and sophisticated Professor is going to be reading their essay. Not likely. Your essay will probably be read by someone on the level of a Teaching Assistant in college. Education in the US tends to be more "relaxed" than around the rest of the world, in my personal opinion. So if you are writing on a very high level you can often sound confusing to the evaluator.

The other problem with writing sentences like this is that Eastern European writers will also often write in the "Passive Voice" instead of the "Active Voice" and so eventually if they keep writing this way, somewhere along the way, they screw up the parallel grammar structure. Or they write something that doesn't make any sense.

Here are two examples:

Active Voice

The woman walked the dog to the store.

Who is doing the action? The woman.

Passive Voice

The dog was walked by the woman to the store.

This is different, the action is happening *to* the dog. This is grammatically correct but when you write essays you can get confused if you add more to the sentence.

So for example if we wrote:

The woman walked the dog to the store and bought dog food.

The sentence makes sense.

But if I wrote:

The dog was walked by the woman to the store and bought dog food.

The sentence doesn't make any sense.

Most people can obviously see the mistakes here but they are less obvious when you are using sophisticated wording. Try to always use the ACTIVE VOICE when writing the essays. You should definitely google "Active Voice" and "Parallel Sentence Structure" to go over these issues. It is worth doing the practice tests online to better understand and avoid these careless mistakes.

PART 3: THE MULTIPLE CHOICE

You may be wondering why this section seems to be so small. Part of why, is that most test takers know exactly what to do in this section. When I get students in my class who have previously failed the test, the majority of them had received 3 pluses on their multiple choice, but they failed the essay section because they ran out of time.

This is why you should always write your essays first.

You will also notice that there are no practice questions in the back of this book. In my opinion it is useless to pad a book with practice multiple choice questions that will not be on your test. There are plenty of practice tests that you can go online and use for free to do this. I recommend the MTEL practice test for English. The MTEL is the Massachusetts Teachers certification exam and I prefer it to the NYSTCE Preparation Guide because it has about 100 questions per practice test. It's free and very similar to the NY tests. I also recommend using practice tests for the ACT because those tests will break down the multiple choice reading comprehension questions into categories. Understanding the type of reading comprehension passage you are reading helps you "frame" your mind to anticipate the kinds of questions you are likely to be given.

But you all already know what to do on a Multiple Choice test. You read the question and you pick the answer. My goal here is to give you a few strategies to use to help streamline this section. For example, most people will read an entire passage and then say "What?" and then go back and read the passage again. This takes up time. So my strategies are based on my observations about the types of passages chosen on timed exams.

A little about me and how I came up with these strategies:

I have taught all different kinds of tests including the ACT, SAT, GRE, and the NYSTCE. I never really realized how good I had gotten in test taking until I went to a job interview several years ago. It was an interview for an SAT English section teacher in a Chinese Tutoring School in Brooklyn. I went down to the interview and was surprised when I walked in, to find several interviewees waiting in a classroom. The director walked in and handed us each a copy of the English section of the SAT and told us we needed to take the test before they would interview us.

Woah! I had not prepared at all and at first it freaked me out. But then I thought, *"Well it makes sense, they want to make sure we can pass it if we're going to teach it. Right?"* I sat down and finished the test in 30 minutes. When I got up the rest of the people in the room were shocked. I went to the counter to turn in the test and they were shocked that I had gotten a perfect score. (I was pretty surprised myself.) I know that I am a very fast reader and that's an asset. So is being hearing impaired; it's very easy for me to focus on an exam. I just take out my hearing aid and bam!....total silence.

They hired me on the spot and then I taught for a summer. At the end of the summer they asked me to come back to teach the same group of kids through the year and I realized, "I've taught them all I know, we're just going to be repeating at this point." So I left the job.

When I told my friends about this story they patted me on the back and called me a genius! I was even invited to a Trivia Night by a group of friends who were excited thinking they had a secret weapon on their team and we'd wipe out the competition. But nope! I only got one question right. It was a question about the Cold War Era.

So this made me wonder why I had done so well on the test. My Master's Degree is in Liberal Studies. It's an unusual degree but it reflects my interests. I focused on comparative mythologies, religion, history, literature and diverse writers. In my undergraduate degree in English I had studied African American writers for two semesters, Ethnic American Writers, Female Writers and Native American Writers. I realized I had read a lot more diverse writers than most people do. But that still didn't answer my question because none of the writers I had studied ever showed up on the test. What was going on?

What I discovered over time is that there is a pattern to the types of passages chosen for the test. And these patterns of passages generally ask the same types of questions. If you know WHY a passage was probably chosen, you will understand what to look for when you are reading the passage.

I have a theory that I will explain to you in the next section. It's a theory that involves race and gender and it's tricky because I don't want people thinking I'm making stereotypes about races or genders. It's not about people, it's about the types of *passages* that are typically chosen on the exam. So bear with me. Then go do a few practice tests and see if the strategy works.

Dead White Men

Most people are surprised when I start off talking about this phrase. They think I invented it myself, but if you google it, you will see an explanation online. Dead White Men is an academic term that reflects the bulk of academic curriculum in the U.S.

Stop and think about your own education in school. If you are older than 30 you will likely have been taught about Dead White Men in the majority of your studies from Elementary School onward. It still applies to younger people as well but the trend has shifted a bit to include more diversity.

Think about what you learned about in History class?

George Washington, Benjamin Franklin, Thomas Jefferson, Abraham Lincoln. *(dead white guys)*

Napoleon, Columbus, Hitler, Stalin, Franklin Delano Roosevelt, Dwight D. Eisenhower, John F. Kennedy etc. *(dead white guys)*

What about Science Class?

Newton, Galileo Galilei, Watson and Crick, Thomas Edison, Alexander Graham Bell, Charles Darwin, Albert Einstein. *(dead white guys)*

Now think about what authors you learned about in your English Classes.

- Shakespeare
- Charles Dickens

- Nathanial Hawthorne
- George Orwell
- John Milton
- John Steinbeck
- Emerson
- Edgar Allen Poe
- J.D Salinger
- William Golding
- Franz Kafka

If you can't remember the authors think of the titles of the literature:

- Romeo and Juliet, Hamlet, Macbeth
- Great Expectations
- The Scarlet Letter
- Animal Farm
- Paradise Lost
- Of Mice and Men
- Self-Reliance
- The Tell Tale Heart, The Raven
- The Catcher in the Rye
- Lord of the Flies
- The Metamorphosis

Think of all the poetry from the Romantic era etc. *Dead white men; Dead white men; Dead white men.*

Since our country has gotten much more diverse over the years, there has been an attempt to reflect that diversity in the curriculum. So you probably have learned about Martin Luther King Jr. and Native Americans as well. You probably also have learned about Marie Curie and Eleanor

Roosevelt. But there is a lack of material from which to make a selection for a reading comprehension passage, because *so few diverse writers were ever published* years ago.

Let's play a game. I want you to stop and think for a second. Let's talk about WHITE WOMEN. Just that little step into diversity. Here we are in 2015 and I want you to stop and think of a powerful white woman in America today. I'll even leave room for you to write it down.

Don't turn the page until you think of one!

Now when I do this in the classroom, almost every single person writes down the same name. "Hillary Clinton." They all laugh and say "wow!" But that's not the interesting part of this question. The interesting part of the question is this: Now think of another one? When I do this in the class many people struggle to think of another one. I've even had people write down "Oprah" or "Michelle Obama" not realizing that these are not white women. Oops.

Think of how strange it is that in 2015 most people can't really list 5 powerful white women or white women authors off the top of their head. If that's what is happening *now* imagine what it was like many years ago?

White women were rarely published years ago. Even today, we can find two books that are extremely successful in their own ways: "Harry Potter" and "Fifty Shades of Grey" and both these female writers published their books with their initials or a pseudonym instead of their full name. J.K. Rowling and E.L. James. J.K. Rowling also published a new book under the pseudonym Robert Galbraith. Interesting, right?

Standardized tests are designed to be academically diverse. And yet, there isn't that much of a selection from which to choose. So it's important to think about why a diverse writer would have been published in the first place. I break it down into three categories.

- Style
- Era
- Diversity

Style

Some writers are just really good writers and so they are selected for their writing itself. For example if I mentioned the white women writers: Emily Dickinson, Jane Austen, and Virginia Woolf. You probably have heard of them, even if you aren't very familiar with their work, you've probably heard of them because they are considered classic female writers. Some writers are "just that good." They are renowned in the field of literature.

In other words, you probably have heard of them because their works were published again and again for each new generation. There's not really a strategy for this, the writing and the questions are straightforward.

Remember they are good writers and the questions are easy to understand. If you have heard of a writer, there's a chance you already have some understanding of who they are, when they wrote and their style of writing. Don't stress when you recognize the name of an author. Keep it Simple.

Era and Dates

When I thought back on why I got the only question right that I did in the Trivia Night game, I realized it was because it had included the date. And this was an important clue. I realized that the reason I tend to do better on Multiple Choice Questions is that when there is a DATE listed, I know how to frame it in history.

Think about how many Reading Comprehension passages you have read, and ask yourself if you ever paid any attention to the DATE? That is a huge clue on a multiple choice test.

Publishing is a business just like any other. Think about if you were in charge of choosing a book or manuscript to be published. What would you look for in the material? You want it to sell! You want to make money! As I write this, it is a few days after the terrorist attack in France. The media is filled with stories about the Syrian refugees. If you had two options of books from which to choose, which book would you choose to publish right now?

Book A: "Journey Through The Wilderness" John Smith

John Smith's book is about his travels through the wilderness of the South Western United States exploring the Native American culture.

Book B: "Steps to Freedom" by Bashir al Khoury

Bashir al Khoury's book is about a refugee escaping the Civil War in Syria and walking through Europe to get to Germany.

Which book would you choose to publish and why? Think about it.

There are certain eras in history that were filled with the same kinds of debates, wars, struggles for freedom and rights. When a book, essay, editorial was published in that era, there's a good chance it was chosen for a political reason. And there's also a good chance that we "kept it on file" all these years later because it reflected an important aspect of that era. The DATE gives you a clue.

Let's consider some eras.

Back to white women again. Generally speaking if you see a white woman's writing on a test it was chosen for one of three reasons:

   A. She's a good writer
   B. She's a scientist
   C. She's a feminist

Female scientists are being included in curriculum more and more because of the issues related to how young women see themselves in the fields of science. You may have heard of the term STEM: Science, Technology, Engineering and Math. Studies over the years have shown a real lack of female role models for young female students. So standardized tests have shifted to reflect this and will often use female scientists who have new theories or ideas.

Always read the information in the heading before you begin reading the passage!

One of the reasons I was very good at taking the timed exams is that I would always read the heading before I began reading the passage. In my case, I didn't even have to read the passage to know the answer because the top part had all the information I needed to know. I do ***not*** recommend this to you. However, I've noticed that most people never read that top part that will give you a better understanding of what you are reading. This is especially important if you do not recognize the name of the author. You should use it to frame your understanding as you read. Let's look at an example.

Read the excerpt below from "A Day in the Life" (1892) by Laura Anderson and answer the questions that follow.

Before I even begin reading I know a few things.

1. She's probably a white woman
2. The date is 1892
3. She's probably a feminist.

How do I know she's probably a white woman? Because most ethnic writers are also identified as such. It will tell you that she's a diverse writer or you can figure it out from their name. Example:

Read the excerpt below from "The Winding Staircase" (1958) by Shanda Morrison, an African American writer, and then answer the questions that follow.

Or

Read the excerpt below from "A Slowly Fading Sunrise" (1971) by Alexandra Chang Johnson, an Asian American writer, and then answer the questions that follow.

How do I know she's a probably a feminist? The date. This is what I mean by Era.

The Suffragette Movement 1840-1920

In 1870 the Fifteenth Amendment was passed which stated that a person could not be denied the right to vote based on their race, color or previous condition of servitude. This was right after the Civil War and it essentially gave black men the right to vote. Now stop and think about how that is going to go over with prominent women in society in that era? They are realizing they need to get the right to vote too. So the first feminist movement took off in the United States. It was formally called the Suffragette movement and started in the late 19th Century lasting into the 20th Century when women finally got the right to vote in 1920 with the Nineteenth Amendment.

Obviously if they are selecting female writers from that era, especially white female writers they are very likely to be feminists. Why? Because that's who got published back then!

Let's consider another era!

Industrialization 1820-1870

Push/Pull

Push refers to reasons people were pushed out of their homeland. Pull refers to why immigrants wanted to move to a different country.

In history there are two major Eras of Industrialization. The first one is when we started growing crops and settling down building cities. The second one is referred to as the New Industrialized Era. When passages are chosen on standardized tests and you can tell that is about working in factories, there's usually a political reason the writing was published.

Back then, we didn't have unions. Factory conditions were dangerous with long hours and little to no protections in place for the workers. Many immigrants who came to the United States and worked in factories at that time, suffered from depression and medical issues because of the unsanitary conditions in the factories. I always tell my students to remember that on a standardized test Industrialization is BAD. It hurt people, reduced them to robots, created respiratory issues and is generally indicted as a horrible period of development in the United States. That's why unions became so important.

It's also important because it relates to the mid-19th century wave of immigrants to the U.S.

The political reason for selecting these passages is to try to challenge the idea that America is this amazing place and that immigrants were running here for opportunity and America, being the *nicest place in the world* took them in and helped them.

It's interesting right now to consider the reaction to the Syrian refugees and compare it to that era. Are Americans today saying "Yes 'give us your tired, your poor, your huddled masses yearning to breathe free!'" Nope! Many people are really suspicious of these refugees and have an attitude that they are "dirty dangerous foreigners" and we shouldn't let them in the United States. Keep this in mind because this is exactly how people reacted in the past.

When the Irish came to the United States because of the potato famine (1845-1852), Americans weren't necessarily sympathetic to the fact that they were literally starving to death over there. They were annoyed and these immigrants were treated poorly. They are the ones who worked most of these miserable factory jobs along with other European immigrants.

If you see a selection that you can identify as being part of that era, it is likely a negative story with criticism of the United States and factories.

The Great Depression 1929-1939

The Great Depression was disastrous time in the United States that came partially as a result of massive industrialization and also as a cost of World War I (1914-1918). When the stock market crashed in 1929, it took the country with it. People struggled to find jobs. President Roosevelt was considered an inspiring leader who tried to keep Americans thinking positively and focusing forward while he created plans of support including the New Deal.

When passages from this era show up on tests it is important to consider that the emotional state of Americans at this time was one of desperation because of so much poverty. Even farms collapsed during this era. It was a time of struggle and sadness in the U.S.

World War II 1939-1945

One of the things that I hope you learn in reading this section, is how similar to the people in the past we are today. Isn't it interesting how the same issues repeat themselves? When you think of history as some far away land in time, you make understanding it much harder than it needs to be. The world has the same types of problems again and again.

Think about how America responded to the War in Iraq. Think about how expensive it was and how this impacted our economy in the years afterward. Now consider how you would feel today if the government said that they wanted to get involved in another war? Many people would say "I don't care, it's not our problem, I'm sick of getting involved in the world's problems when we have enough of our problems here at home." This was a similar sentiment during World War II.

When the U.S. finally got involved in World War II it actually helped out economy because we started building weapons, tanks, and other military equipment. Women started working in factories while the men went to war. You may remember seeing pictures of "Rosie the Riveter" as an icon of the way women got involved in helping here at home. When the war ended we had gotten very good at building weapons. And this put us in a very precarious position. If the US is the country that has the strongest military, then what is going to be expected of us in the future when there are other times a military force is needed to intervene on behalf of other countries and the United Nations?

At the end of World War II we found ourselves in a good economic position but many people were fatigued from the idea of war. Many women were tired of working in factories and wanted to return to more traditional roles like homemakers and mothers. They wanted to focus on families and building a nice home life. And so they did, which is why the generation born in this era is known as the "baby boom" generation.

The Civil Rights Movement 1955-1968

This era is one that is generally known to most test takers. The writers were usually political and talking about the issues related to segregation in schools and equal rights. You should easily be able to understand what these passages are about. In general they deal with topics about racial discrimination in the U.S.

You should also try to familiarize yourself with eras that involve other important political issues in history. But keep in mind that this is a standardized teaching certification exam. On standardized exams in general, they don't want to choose passages that are very controversial because it could be a form of bias. So don't feel that you need to know all of the political debates in history. I have chosen the eras above because I realize these are ones with which test takers in my class are the least familiar.

You should note, that although modern standardized tests strive to be more diverse, you *will see* White Male writers on the test. In general they are included when they are discussing topics about technologies, innovations or new ways of seeing things. Don't make the mistake of thinking all the writers on the test will be diverse.

One last suggestion I want to give you is to familiarize yourself with important speeches in history. When "Dead White Men" are chosen for these tests they often use historical speeches because they reflect some of the eras mentioned above and the way the world was changing. Presidential Speeches are very often used on any standardized exam. They are important to know.

Diversity

This section, again, is a tricky one. I don't want readers to think I am promoting stereotypes about ***people***. Just remember that I am talking about typical patterns in ***passages*** that were chosen for publication. These passages are often from many decades ago and so they don't necessarily reflect the modern world. This is why I have pointed out that paying attention to dates is very important.

For example there is a very big difference between the kind of writing an African American author would write today as compared to one writing in the 1950s or even the 1980s. So keep in mind some of these ideas when reading the passages. And remember, these are all based on my own opinion and observations of patterns.

Black Writers in History

You might wonder why I haven't written African American writers. This is because not all black writers are African American and it is important to understand the distinction in the passages on the exam.

Most historic African American writers have lived in a racist country their entire lives. I know a lot of people will say, *"Wait, it's not that bad, I'm not racist, America has changed!"* And that might be true for you, but it doesn't change the reality of racism in the United States. Racism is not the same thing as prejudice.

Racism is an ***institution***, not simply someone being discriminatory of a person because of their race. That's why when you hear people making the statement, "that's reverse racism!" you know they don't understand what racism really means. The term racism is used so casually today that most people say "racism" when they really mean "discrimination based on race" or "prejudice."

So what does racism mean? Our country, unfortunately has a long history of creating systems that deny African Americans the ability to form an ***identity*** in this country. These systems are woven into the fabric of our country and started with slavery and carried through into voting, employment, education, the ability to buy a house or rent an apartment, living conditions etc. It has gone on for decades despite attempts to reconcile the inequity.

Part of the problem with denying someone's ability to build an identity, is that people are expected to assimilate to the majority in the country. Since the majority in our country is white, this became the standard by which all other cultures were expected to conform. This is sometimes referred to as the "tyranny of the majority." It also influenced the kinds of writers that were chosen for publication and the way in which African American history was also overlooked throughout the years.

This denial of identity can show up in casual ways even the 21rst century. For example, consider the television show **Friends**. This show was supposedly about a group of friends living in NYC. Yet not only were all of them white, they very rarely met any other ethnic group on the show. The show was criticized for "white washing" NYC. Anyone who lives in NYC knows that it is diverse. But on **Friends**, the only black character that ever showed up was played by Aisha Tyler for a few episodes.

What does that tell the African American community? It says, "You are invisible, you don't really matter, you don't count."

If this is going on in the 21rst century, imagine what was going on in the past? Ralph Ellison wrote an award winning novel entitled <u>The Invisible Man</u> that addressed this issue. Passages written by African American writers in general on standardized tests, will have been ***chosen*** for the way that their writing addresses this issue. When reading these types of passages keep in mind the date and what was going on at that point in history as it related to racism.

Immigrant Black Writers

Now imagine coming to the United States as a black person from Jamaica, West Indies, Haiti, Barbados, The Bahamas or countries in Africa. Think about the difference of someone growing up in a country where their identity was not denied. Instead it was celebrated and developed. Now imagine that person coming to the United States and experiencing racism that denies identity on a regular basis. It is a drastic form of culture shock.

Actor Sidney Poitier, who grew up in The Bahamas, moved to Florida when he was 15 years old. This is what he said about his experience:

"I didn't run into racism until we moved to Nassau when I was ten and a half, but it was vastly different from the kind of horrendous oppression that black people in Miami were under when I moved there at 15. I found Florida an antihuman place. But by the time I got there, I already had a sense of myself – I knew who I was. And I was of value. So when Florida said to me, 'You are not who you think you are,' I said, 'Oh, yes I am. I am who I think I am. I am not who you think I am.'"

Sidney Poitier did not move back to The Bahamas, instead he moved to New York City and got involved in acting and today is an Oscar winning actor who is very well respected.

His experience is one that helps us understand the difference between immigrant black writers and African American writers. As immigrants, they come to the United States with the hope of building a successful life just like any other immigrant. But the transition is often conflicting and confusing because of the reality of life here.

Jamaican writer Claude McKay wrote a poem about this experience in 1921. It is called "America."

Although she feeds me bread of bitterness,
And sinks into my throat her tiger's tooth,
Stealing my breath of life, I will confess
I love this cultured hell that tests my youth.
Her vigor flows like tides into my blood,
Giving me strength erect against her hate,
Her bigness sweeps my being like a flood.
Yet, as a rebel fronts a king in state,
I stand within her walls with not a shred
Of terror, malice, not a word of jeer.
Darkly I gaze into the days ahead,
And see her might and granite wonders there,
Beneath the touch of Time's unerring hand,
Like priceless treasures sinking in the sand.

This is a common theme in the experience of immigrant black writers. They are conflicted between the love of the country and the racism they experience here. It is a very strange place to get used to and they often become homesick even though they wish to stay.

Asian American Themes

Asian writers and themes in the writing generally center around the difference between traditional cultures and what it is like to grow up in a more modern generation. For example, if you have seen the movie "The Joy Luck Club" which is based on a novel by Amy Tan, you will remember that the story was about four modern Asian daughters and their relationships with their traditional Asian mothers.

The traditional Asian home is one of pride, success, decency and a respect for one's "elders." This is very different in the modern American world, where "youth" tends to get more attention. Asian writers often discuss the struggles between the elder's sadness at watching the abandonment of their traditions and the younger generation's attempts to succeed in a less traditional world.

Native American Themes

Most test takers are familiar with these themes because they learn about them in school. However I notice that many writers confuse the spiritual beliefs of Native Americans with that of Hindus or Buddhists. Native Americans believe in "animism" which is a belief that the Universe and all it contains, has souls or spirits. This is why in history many Native Americans refused to move away from their homelands. They felt a connection to the spirits or souls in that region. The "Trail of Tears" is an event in history where many Native Americans died in a forced removal from their homeland.

Native American writers will often write about the way their traditions and cultures were not understood by Europeans and White Americans. These writers are often noted for their "voice" in writing because they have a very unique style of expression. Themes in these passages celebrate their traditions and examine the way racism has hurt their community.

Types of Reading Comprehension Passages

When I taught the ACT and the SAT one of the strategies I taught students was to make sure they understood the different types of Reading Comprehension Passages that show up on the test. Now that you know how to analyze the eras and diversity of writers, you also want to pay attention to the types of passages you will get and the kinds of questions generally associated with them. A good way to be able to see the differences in these types of passages is to take a free practice ACT online. On those tests they identify the different type of passages.

Prose Fiction:

Short stories or excerpts from larger fiction texts. In general the questions for these types of passages are divided into two different categories.

- Character motivation questions
- Author's purpose questions

Character motivation questions are about how the character feels, behaves or reacts to a situation.

Author's purpose questions are related to stylistic choices made by the writer, metaphor, simile, using juxtaposition (putting two examples next to each other for comparison or contrast) and understanding the author's goal in using these writing styles.

Social Science Passages:

Social science passages are generally related to culture. When reading Social Science Passages always identify the culture being discussed as a way of framing and understanding what the passage is describing. Most Social Science passages on these types of tests are evaluating for understanding a "protected class" in America (African Americans, Feminists, Asian Americans, Native Americans, Hispanic, etc.) to be sure that a reader has a good understanding of the struggles of minorities in the world.

These types of passages are often eye opening in understanding a culture. There is an expression that says "The victors write the history." This means true history is not always documented the way it happened, but instead is a biased version of what happened. A good example of this is the way in the past, young people were taught that Christopher Columbus discovered America. The truth is, that Christopher Columbus never set foot in America in his life. He only ever landed in the Caribbean islands. Social Science passages are usually about History, Anthropology and Social issues. They want the reader to evaluate the information and be able to address problems and misconceptions and new ideas.

Opinionated Essays or Editorial Essays:

These types of excerpts usually are written as a persuasive type of essay. Generally the writer will take on a previously held view and challenge it. The writing will usually be written in a casual and less "academic" voice because the author is trying to convince the average person to reconsider a previously held belief. These types of essays will use anecdotal stories as a way of "hooking" the reader in the introduction. The questions related to them will ask the reader to evaluate the thought process of the author and to demonstrate an understanding of how the author develops their idea. You will often be asked about how the writer transitions between ideas.

Science Passages:

Science passages will ask readers to evaluate data presented in the passage. The goal of testing for a science passage is to make sure the reader understands details and can also infer other information presented. These passages test to make sure the reader is able to discern the evidence the author uses to make their point.

These passages also encourage readers to understand the author's point of view, since most science writers are proposing a theory. Theorists will put forth a theory and then give several examples to back up their claims. Usually science writers will alternate between anecdotal (personal experiences) and science to back up their claims. When identifying Science passages look for medical terminology, biology and environmental sciences as a topic. Usually these are Science passages.

Technological or Educational type passages:

These types of passages are similar to "Science" passages because the writer has a theory regarding technology or education. They typically present a unique perspective in reexamining preexisting ideas or systems. The questions are testing for inferential and literal comprehension. They will ask for details as well as critical analysis.

Keep in mind the difference between a literal question and an inferential one.

- Literal question

The answer is found directly in the passage.

- Inferential question

The reader has to "infer" or figure out what the writer is saying.

Tips to Remember

- The questions usually go in order through the passage. If a question identifies the line number, the *next* question will likely ask about information right after it.
- When referred to a line number be sure to also read the sentence before and after that line to be sure you understand the sentence.
- Vocabulary word questions are easier to figure out if you use the context of the sentence to analyze the meaning.
- Most people do not fail the multiple choice section. This means it is not a hard section. Don't stress.
- Make sure you don't waste time if you really don't understand a question, just make an educated guess and move on. You will run out of time. There's

probably always one question you won't get right. Don't waste time on it.
- **NEVER CHANGE YOUR ANSWERS.**
- Statistically it has been proven that your odds lower if you change an answer. If you are debating between two answers, stick with your original choice. You should only change an answer if you are 100 percent sure that the one you originally chose is wrong.

Remember when you take your test that you should do it in this order.

A. Write the essays
B. Do the Multiple Choice
C. Edit the Essay.

Now go take your test! Good Luck

And remember to BAKE YOUR COOKIES!

You must practice writing if you want to pass the exam!

Remember to relax as much as possible. **It's just a test**, the only bad thing that can happen is that you have to pay to take it again and you wasted time and money. These tests are hard and they are asking you to get a very high score. Not passing a test doesn't mean you are not an intelligent person. It just means you are not that good at taking tests. And always consider how this will help you be a better teacher because you will understand first-hand the difficulties your own students may have with the same issues.

We hope this book has been helpful in giving you a better understanding of the ALST. And, as always, we are in classes every Sunday teaching test prep for the NYSTCE. We teach the EAS, CST Students with Disabilities and the CST Multi Subject as well. We also have a video and strategy workshop to help you prepare for your EdTPA. And I, Bridgette, personally really appreciate it if you can give this book a review on Amazon.

Thank you for letting me be your coach!

Feel free to find us online at brooklynedu.org

Or email at brooklynedu@gmail.com

Made in the USA
Middletown, DE
31 December 2016